FORENSIC SCIENCE

Crime Scene Analysis

DAVID ELIO MALOCCO,

B.C.L., B.Sc., Dip. P.C.P., Dip. F. Sc.

ISBN: 149939876X
ISBN-13: 978-1499398762

DEDICATION

This book is dedicated to my mother Margaret, my wife Colette and my cousin, Psychiatrist James I. Hannon, M.D. and his wife Psychologist Dr. Noelle Hannon, both of Park Avenue, New York, New York.

CONTENTS

Acknowledgments I

1 Introduction Page 3

2 Crime Scene – An Overview Page 6

3 Crime Scene Recognition Page 9

4 Documenting a Crime Scene Page 12

5 What a CSI Team Looks For Page 20

6 Fingerprints Page 29

7 Firearms and Ballistics Page 37

8 Documents and Computers Page 45

9 Causes of Death – The Autopsy Page 46

10 Identifying Skeletons Page 55

11 Identifying Decaying Bodies Page 68

12 Poisons Page 78

13 Fraud: Disputed Documents Page 83

14 Cyber Crime Page 92

15 DNA Page 106

16 Committing the Perfect Crime Page 112

17 Glossary of Terms Page 120

18 Bibliography Page 131

ACKNOWLEDGMENTS

To the Arts Council of Ireland.

1 INTRODUCTION

"Society wants to believe it can identify evil people, or bad or harmful people, but it's not practical. There are no stereotypes." Ted Bundy, *Convicted Serial Killer now executed.*

The television crime series *CSI* which premiered on the American network CBS on the 6 October 2000, is one of the world's most popular television programs. By 2002 it was the most watched show on American television spawning not one, but two spin-offs, namely *CSI: Miami* and *CSI: New York*. Incidentally, CSI stands for Crime Scene Investigation. This series and numerous other crime programs have been criticized for "teaching criminals how to avoid getting caught." But just how accurate are the programs?

The answer is that that they are not very accurate. There is no typical crime scene. Each one is disparate. Neither is there a common body of evidence to be extracted from each scene. The reality is that each investigation will be conducted in a different manner.

So, let's dispel some of those Hollywood myths. To begin with Forensic Science is not magic. No CS investigator is going to go into a crime scene, pick up a single strand of hair from the victim, bring it back to the lab, scan it in a green machine, process it into his computer and come out with an image of its owner's driving license twenty four hours later. Firstly, they have to find a match for the hair. If its owner has no criminal record and doesn't work in a State job there will be no match. Even if there is a match it doesn't mean guilt, just contact. Finally, the process takes weeks not hours.

Another common myth is that in not talking to the police you are obstructing the course of justice and committing a felony. I don't think so. Americans are protected by the Fifth Amendment and most civilized countries also have protection against self-incrimination. What this means is that, under no circumstances, can you be coerced into being a witness against yourself. And, since at the moment the police speak to you, you do not know if you're a suspect or not, that means you always have the right to not talk to the police.

This should not be confused with obstruction of justice which is completely different. This arises when you tell lies to the police, destroy evidence or otherwise intentionally try to sabotage their investigation. But simply refusing to talk to them is not a crime. Having said that, in most countries the police do have the right to ask you to identify yourself and you must tell them. In America this is covered by the 1972 Supreme Court case *Nebraska vs Heywood Jablome.*

This book will show you exactly what the police will and will not do and specifically what happens at a crime scene, or at least, what is supposed to happen. It will also show you how the process evolves so as to capture the culprit. Can a criminal, by studying the techniques involved in crime scene analysis and subsequent forensic tests, avoid capture? Yes, it is possible in so far as knowledge of the process will reduce the risk of conviction. But please accept that this book is not meant to be a bible to assist criminals commit the perfect crime.

If you have none or very little experience of how investigators and police forces conduct their investigations you will be surprised at how technology has advanced to assist them. You will be equally surprised at how a clever offender can easily thwart those investigations.

This book is written as an introductory guide for anyone undertaking study in crime scene analysis and forensic science; for existing police enforcement officers; for criminal lawyers; and for those writers of crime fiction who need to bring themselves up to date with new procedures and techniques. But in actual fact, the book is for anyone interested in crime.

The first part of the book will deal with crime scene analysis, that is, what happens at the crime scene. The second part deals with forensic science, where the information and evidence gathered at the crime scene is further examined by experts in the laboratory.

In practical terms, depending on the police enforcement agency involved, there can be an overlap between personnel at both the crime scene and the laboratory. But, in *Forensic Science – Crime Scene Analysis*, each expert function will be examined separately for the purposes of clarity.

People are fascinated by crime in general and murder in particular, hence, the proliferation of crime programs on television and in film. During lectures and seminars I have noticed that the two most popular questions attendees ask are: "Is it possible to commit the perfect crime? And, "What is the perfect murder weapon?"

The answers are all here but first, let's deal with what happens when police get called to the scene of a crime.

2 CRIME SCENES – AN OVERVIEW

"How often have I said to you that when you have eliminated the impossible, whatever remains, however improbable, must be the truth?"
Sherlock Holmes, *The Sign of Four*.

A crime scene can be defined as the location which is linked to the commission of a crime.

Who is the first person at the crime scene? It's not the police nor the crime scene investigators. It's the offender and if there is one, the victim. The police arrive after the crime has been committed. If the offender is still there he will be arrested. Even if he confesses to the crime, is arrested and charged, evidence must be acquired to substantiate the confession. This is because many people admit to crimes they have not committed.

There are also cases where police enforcement agencies have used undue influence on a suspect causing them to admit to a crime. You even have occasions when someone genuinely believes they have committed a crime but, in fact, have not. Accordingly, the collection of evidence; the proper logging of evidence; the correct storing and analysis of evidence is vital in any criminal case.

Once the police arrive at a crime scene they are responsible for securing the scene to prevent any evidence being destroyed. The Crime Scene Investigators are then called in to examine the scene in detail. Where necessary, a legal adviser will be called in to decide if search warrants are required. If they are required then the legal adviser is obliged to make an application to a judge to obtain them. In the event of a death then the appropriate medical examiner will attend. Usually, this will be a medical doctor trained in forensic pathology.

In the event that a particular death requires expert analysis then experts such as entomologists, forensic scientists and forensic psychologists will be called in to assist in the investigation but not necessarily to the actual crime scene.

The division of labor between the police and the crime scene investigators is clear. The crime scene investigators analyze the physical evidence at the crime scene. The police, on the other hand, interview witnesses. The CS investigators examine the physical evidence; the police examine the witnesses and the leads provided by the evidence. Both parties work together to ensure the conviction of the correct offender.

Usually, the system works like this. The police call the CS investigators. They arrive and secure the crime scene. Although the police should also take steps to ensure that the scene is cordoned off. The CS investigators carry out an initial walk through to get an overall feel of the crime. They question the attendant police to ascertain if anything has been moved by them. They then generate their initial opinions on the crime. They may make a note of potential evidence but at this initial stage they don't usually disturb anything.

The next stage is for the CS investigators to document everything. This will be done by sketches, photographs and video. The scene as a whole is forensically documented. The purpose of this is to capture the crime scene prior to any evidence being disturbed. Simple things like touching and moving evidence can seriously prejudice a potential conviction. Nothing is touched during the documenting stage. There are some exceptions to this, where, for example, the medical examiner requests a body to be turned over for documenting.

Why is it necessary to document so thoroughly? Because

eventually evidence will become contaminated. Rain will wash away blood stains; furniture will be moved in the search for a weapon and to examine blood spatter; items will be removed for analysis; in short, nothing will remain the same.

It is only now that the CS investigators begin to touch things. They will, of course, be wearing protective clothing (including footwear) and protective gloves so as not to contaminate anything.

They now carry out a systematic detailed search. All potential evidence will be collected, tagged, logged and packaged. It is important that the evidence remains intact en-route to the laboratory.

The evidence collected by the CS investigators is delivered to the laboratory when it is forensically examined by experts. Sometimes such experts include members of the CSI team. But usually CS investigators who work in the field do not also work in the laboratories. Even where this is the case, the CS investigators must be sufficiently experienced to recognize the specific value of potential evidence at the scene. For example, they are likely to have some expertise in firearms and fingerprints to understand the potential evidentiary significance of them but are unlikely to have expertise in blood spatter and serology (blood and body fluids).

The tests carried out by the forensic scientists are then delivered to the lead detective on the case. Why is the examination of the crime scene so important? Firstly, it provides us with an interpretation of the circumstances in which the offence has occurred. This, in turn, will help determine the possible type and location of evidence that needs to be collected. Secondly, once collected, this evidence will be used to convict the offender.

3 CRIME SCENE RECOGNITION

"The world is full of obvious things which nobody by any chance ever observes."
Sherlock Holmes, *The Hound of the Baskervilles.*

The first function of the CS investigator is to ascertain what the particular investigation will require and to establish a procedure to discover and collect evidence. So, they must, first of all, establish what constitutes the crime scene. This is not as straightforward as it may appear and will vary according to the particular crime involved.

If police are investigating a murder which has been committed in an apartment then the crime scene might simply be the apartment. But, it may also include the immediate area outside and even the exterior of the building if, for example, a car has been involved. If there is a blood trail on the road and proceeding down the street then that also becomes part of the crime scene. So, instead of the crime scene comprising of the actual apartment it might now extend to the entire neighborhood.

THE EXTENT OF CRIME SCENES

Various law enforcement manuals set out what can constitute a crime scene. In Britain the *ACPO Murder Investigation Manual* provides a comprehensive list and advises that a crime scene can include any or all of the following places:

1. Places where the crime was planned.

2. Places where meetings took place between the victim and offender.

3. Places where the offender detained a victim.

4. Vehicles used in the commission of the crime.

5. The place where a victim's body has been disposed.

6. Weapons used in the crime.

7. Disposal sites of weapons involved in the crime.

8. Places used for the disposal or cleaning of material used in or obtained during the course of the crime.

9. Routes used by the offender going to and from the crime.

10. People who may have come into contact with a suspect or a crime scene. This includes witnesses, victims, suspects and their homes, places of employment and vehicles.

The police usually cordon off the core area and leave the larger areas to be cordoned off to the CS investigators. The reason for this is that it is easier to decrease the size of the crime scene rather than increase it after it has been contaminated.

The scene is ideally secured with tape and unnecessary personnel should be removed from the area. This might even include detectives and police officers. The most important objective is the preservation of evidence.

Once the crime scene is secured a legal adviser will determine if it is necessary to obtain a search warrant. If a search warrant isn't obtained, and should have been, then any evidence gathered will be inadmissible, irrespective of how valuable it may be to the prosecution case. An experienced CS investigator will wait until he gets the all clear from the legal adviser to continue the search.

PRIORITIES AT A CRIME SCENE

The first responder or police officer to attend should call for assistance at once. His primary duty is the preservation of life. If he comes to a crime scene where a person is badly injured he must, first of all, render what assistance he can to that injured party and call for medical assistance.

If the ambulance arrives and takes away an injured party the officer will need to have noted the exact position of the body before its removal. If there is a body at the crime scene then the body must not be touched or moved in any way until such time as it has first been examined by a medical officer and photographed.

CODE OF PRACTICE

Most countries have a code of practice relating to the investigation of a crime scene, the personnel involved and the chain of evidence. In England and Wales the code is the *Code of Practice under the criminal Procedure and Investigations Act 1996*. It sets out clear responsibilities for the personnel involved in an investigation and the maintenance of the chain of evidence.

Most serious investigations would have a crime scene manager. Their duties would include: the provision of a focal point or safe area for the proper management of the scene; assessment of resource requirements and prioritization procedures; health, safety and welfare issues; the recording of evidence recovery plans the documenting actions at the scene.

4 DOCUMENTING A CRIME SCENE

"The term 'holistic' refers to my conviction that what we are concerned with here is the fundamental interconnectedness of all things. I do not concern myself with such petty things as fingerprint powder, telltale pieces of pocket fluff and inane footprints. I see the solution to each problem as being detectable in the pattern and web of the whole. The connections between causes and effects are often much more subtle and complex than we with our rough and ready understanding of the physical world might naturally suppose."
Douglas Adams, *Dirk Gently's Holistic Detective Agency*

Once the crime scene is secure the CS investigator will take an immediate note of all those things which are likely to change over a short period of time.

These will include the weather; is it raining; is it dark and what is the street lighting like? What time of day is it? Is it warm and humid or cold or freezing? Are there any particular smells or aromas that seem unusual, like decomposition, excessive gas, dripping water, or smoke. Are any alarms, like smoke or intruder alarms going off?

He will take a note of what forensic experts will be required. He will take a note of physical things inside the crime area which appear unusual, such as furniture which has been moved, or valuables that are missing.

It is at this stage that one might hear the term the "golden hour principle." This refers to the principle that effective early action can result in securing significant evidential material that would otherwise be lost to the investigation. The collection of such evidence often results in fast track actions. Fast track actions can be defined as any investigative actions which, if pursued immediately, can establish important facts, preserve evidence or lead to the early capture of the offender.

He may require specialist equipment or specific experts to deal with blood spatter and ballistics. He may require the assistance of an entomologist, a serologist, a pathologist, an anthropologist, a forensic artist or sculptor or an odontologist. He will interview first responders (police officers) to the scene to ascertain if they removed or touched or, in any way, interfered with anything at the scene. He may check the telephone to see if there were any recent calls made or received or any messages left.

As soon as CS investigators have completed their plan to gather the relevant evidence the next stage is the documentation of that evidence. In this way, all those parties who did not attend the original crime scene will be able to benefit from its re-construction.

Documentation of the crime scene is effected in four ways; photography, sketching, video and note taking. The aim here is to create a visual record which will assist others to recreate an accurate picture of the crime scene.

CRIME SCENE SKETCHING

A sketch artist is often employed to accurate portray the scene including dimensions and the locations of physical evidence in relation to each other. The artist will depict the location of approaches such as roads, paths, windows, entrances and exits. The sketches will include accurate measurements with the compass direction of north indicated clearly on the sketch.

Rooms will be measured and the location of furniture in those rooms will be set out and distances measured. The goal is to show locations of evidence and how each piece of evidence relates to the rest of the scene. The sketch artist is likely to record details like the height of a door frame, the exact size of the room, the distance from the window to the door and (in a shooting) the location of any bullet holes. Such an expert is likely to use CAD or computer-aided drafting which produces the geographical representation of complex crimes scenes and can facilitate such details as blood spatters.

VIDEO WALK THROUGH

Major cases or cases involving multiple murders or serial killings may also require a video walk through. Such a recording is excellent for providing a good feel for the layout of the crime scene. It can give an accurate view of the time involved in getting from one location to another and what obstacles and turns are involved in that journey.

It is also a good way to catch something which may have been overlooked at the initial investigation because, at the time, investigators were not then aware that they should be looking for it. A video walk through will record the entire crime scene and the surroundings from various different angles. The video will include a constant audio narrative.

PHOTOGRAPHY

We have all seen television programs where a photographer is present at the scene of the crime taking photographs, nearly always, exclusively of the body. In reality, these are no ordinary snappers. These are highly skilled forensic photographers whose evidence is a crucial part of any criminal trial, for both the prosecution and the defense.

Their work is an integral part of the criminal investigation. Photography is essential to capture an accurate account of that which cannot be altered. Photographs are taken solely within a legal context to provide an accurate visual record of an accident or crime scene. They don't just photograph dead bodies. They photograph entire crime scenes, gunshot wounds, bite marks, weapons, trace evidence and even autopsies.

They take pictures of mail and newspapers to help establish dates of death and also photograph documents. However, only original documents can be submitted to a laboratory for analysis. Photography is used instead of photocopiers to make copies of documents. The reason for this is that pressure exerted by the photocopier may damage the original document and any indented writing, fingerprints, trace evidence, erasures or obliterations.

The role of the forensic photographer is to provide accurate, detailed, permanent visual records of accident and crime scenes. Photographs taken must faithfully record the location and evidence as clearly and as objectively as possible. Forensic photographers are obliged to follow a standard methodology. They must produce images to a rigorous technical standard. It is important that they work without disturbing the evidence or interfering with other investigators. Their photographs must be detailed and will include photographs as diverse as tire marks, fingerprints, footprints, blood spatters, bullet holes and other unique evidence. This is all in addition to photographs of dead bodies to record how the body was found, its position when discovered and the nature of its injuries.

Forensic photographers will be *au fait* with such non-standard techniques such as high-intensity and low level aerial imaging, as well as an appreciation of the importance of their work. They must also pay close attention to detail. They need to be able to select and use the best equipment and techniques for the job in all environments and lighting conditions. The photographs they take must be correctly lit and exposed, have maximum depth of field, be free from distortion and be in sharp focus.

The reason why an ordinary professional photographer would be ill-prepared for such an assignment is that forensic photographers require an in-depth understanding of police methods and conventions as well as a sound understanding of anatomy.

Photographs must be objective and not appeal to the emotions of a jury. They are also required to retain detailed records of exactly where photographs were taken, the type of camera and lenses, what stock the picture was taken on, and whether flash or artificial lights were used.

The majority of law enforcement agencies will already have standard photographic kits ready for use at the scene of a crime which will contain all the equipment which might be needed for recording the scene. The kit is likely to include a single-lens reflex camera, for black and white and color photography, both indoor and outdoor. It will also have close up and wide angle lenses, flash equipment, back up batteries, instant Polaroid camera and video recording equipment.

The kits may also contain spare films, tripods, filters, tape measures and specially marked rulers which are laid alongside objects and impressions being photographed, as an indication of size and angle distortion. These rulers are used when photographing injuries sustained by a victim in order to indicate scale and perspective. The photographs will be taken in color.

In some case, particularly in America, photographs of sexual assaults may be excluded if the defense can persuade the judge that the photographs are inflammatory or are such as their opening to the jury is likely to prejudice the accused.

The typical film used for forensic purposes is standard 35mm film. Black and white film, good for documenting contrast differences, or color film may be used depending on the aspects of the scene being photographed.

Forensic photographers also use a special type of film which is only sensitive to infra–red heat for use in appropriate circumstances. There is a special technique for situations where the photographer has no light. This technique is useful outdoors at night, perhaps at the scene of a road traffic accident, or in situations where the room is too big to light or there is no light available for pictures to be taken such as a burned out building in cases of arson.

What type of photographs should a forensic photograph take? Basically, they should take a photograph of everything before it is touched or moved. Not only that, but they should take three different types of shot; overviews, mid-views, and close-ups.

Overview shots are the widest possible views of the entire scene. In the event that the crime scene is inside such shots will include views of all rooms (not just the room where the crime seems to have occurred), with photos taken from each corner and, if a boom is present, overhead; views of the exterior of the building where the crime happened, including photos of all entrances and exits; exterior shots of the building showing its relation to surrounding structures and even photographs of any spectators at the scene

The mid-range photographs should show key pieces of evidence in context, so the photograph includes not only the evidence but also its location in a room and its distance from other pieces of evidence.

Finally, the forensic photograph will take very clear and

distinct close-up shots of individual pieces of evidence. Such close ups should identify any serial numbers or other identifying characteristics. This is where the ruler comes in.

All photographs taken should be placed in a logbook and each individual photograph should have a number, a description of the object or scene in the photograph, the location of the object or scene, the time and date the photograph was taken and any other descriptive details that might be relevant. If there were no descriptions on the photographs then where they are those of a wound a defense attorney could raise doubt as to whether they were entry or exit wounds.

NOTE TAKING

This is not as simple as it seems and should only be undertaken by someone trained in the art of scientific observation. What at first might appear to be blood underneath a dead body may in fact be blood, or decomposition fluid or a mixture of each. Note makers don't make assumptions; they record what they see without analyzing it or drawing conclusions from what they see.

In 2012 a company called Visionations became the first company to introduce an iPad app called *CrimePad* which is designed to assist investigators in crime scene analysis. *CrimePad* is a tool for making a complete electronic record of a crime scene. As no two crime scenes are ever the same how can an app address this problem? In *CrimePad*, data is entered only once, at the scene itself when the information has the highest fidelity to reality, and is used to generate labels, crime scene reports, access logs, evidence logs, and all the other documentation required. It also allows you to relate different objects and locations in a way which isn't possible in the current manual process. Local police departments in California, Virginia, and Tennessee were the first states to use the app but it is now used by at least twenty others. Visionations state that the app is being constantly updated and refined. For example, a new feature which will allow investigators at a scene to call on remote experts in real time. Instead of the consultation with an expert happening at the lab, it can happen at the scene itself. This will allow evidence which would otherwise be overlooked or impossible to retrieve to be collected. Another advantage is that the use of remote experts also means having fewer people at the scene itself, reducing the possibility of contamination.

CrimePad has already been used by CS investigators to share relevant information from the crime scene with criminal investigators in real time.

Currently, it can take days to identify even a simple fingerprint, so the ultimate aim for *CrimePad* is real-time analysis of evidence performed at the scene itself and linked to various police systems and databases.

Eventually, CS investigators have to produce evidence which is admissible in court so the company provide training materials covering not just the use of the application itself, but how to introduce the application into court. Since *CrimePad* was released in 2013, several cases in which it was used have gone through the court process, but the use of an iPad app for documenting evidence is still novel in most courtrooms. However, it is an indication of what will take place in the future.

5 WHAT A CSI TEAM LOOKS FOR

"The criminal is the creative artist: the detective only the critic."
G.K Chesterton, *The Blue Cross*

The function of crime scene investigators is to locate, collect, log and preserve all physical evidence that might help to recreate the crime and identify the culprit in a manner which will comply with court rules on evidence.

The type of physical evidence they will look for will include trace evidence, impressions, fluids, fibers, weapons and documents.

Trace evidence comprises of such items as gunshot residue, broken glass, drugs, unknown chemicals and paint residue. Impressions primarily consist of fingerprints but also include footprints and tool marks. They will look for hair and fibers, particularly those which are alien to the crime scene and might have come from the offender. In the event of injury they will check for guns, knives, bullets, bullet holes and cartridge casings.

Documents can provide very worthwhile and relevant evidence so they will look at diaries, suicide notes, phone books, crumpled paper in trash cans as well as electronic information like computers, hard drives, mobile phones and answering machines. Finally, they will search for four types of body fluid, blood, semen, saliva and vomit.

If there is a body at the scene of the crime a preliminary examination might be carried out *in situ* or the body may be brought away for an autopsy. In either case the body is photographed first before being touched. They will then carry out a visual examination of the body, primarily to ascertain the cause of death.

Before the body is moved from the scene they will usually examine the following:

Are there any stains or marks on the clothing?
Is the clothing bunched up which might indicate dragging?
What bruises, abrasion or wounds are on the body?
Are there defensive wounds?
Is there anything missing from the body such as items of clothing or jewelry?

Where there is a significant amount of blood at or near the body they will check to see if the direction of the blood flow is consistent with the laws of gravity. If it isn't then the body may have been moved. If there is very little blood or no blood pool then it may indicate that the victim was killed elsewhere and brought to a different place post-mortem. Are there any bodily fluids present at or near the blood pool? If there is evidence of insect activity then they know they will require the expertise of a forensic entomologist to determine how long the victim is dead.

Once the body has been examined by the medical officer it is usually prepared for transportation. Technicians will wrap the body in a white cloth and put paper bags over the hands and feet. The reason for this is to preserve any trace evidence on the victim.

Items worth checking for at a crime scene include:

Cigarette butts: These are perfect for picking up DNA samples.
Door and Windows: Are they open or shut or have they been forced?
Mail: Has the mail been interfered with?
Furniture: Is there any evidence of a struggle?
Kitchen: Is there any uneaten or partially eaten food or used cups or glasses?

Toilets: If the apartment belongs to a sole female occupant is the toilet seat up?

Trash cans: These will always be checked.

Bathroom: Are all the towels there? Have any been used to clean up? Are there any blood stains in the sink or bath?

Shooting: Each bullet, each shell and each hole will be examined and identified.

Stabbing: Are any knives missing from the kitchen?

Impressions: Are there any footprints on the floors or outside? Are there tire marks in the driveway.

Walls and ceilings: Are there any blood spatters visible?

Note that forensic personnel will also have specialized equipment to determine if blood has been recently cleaned up and to discover blood invisible to the naked eye. They will use luminol and a portable UV light to reveal blood that has been washed off a surface.

LUMINOL

Luminol is the killer's curse. Much of forensic science is based on the principle that nothing vanishes without a trace. This is particularly so in murder cases. Even if the killer disposes of a body; cleans up the blood at the scene with a heavy duty detergent, and burns the cleaning cloths, the likelihood is that some evidence will still remain.

You can clean, clean, clean but some tiny particles of blood will cling to most surfaces for years and years, without anyone ever knowing that they are there.

The basic idea of luminol is to reveal these traces with a light-producing chemical reaction between several chemicals and hemoglobin. Hemoglobin is an oxygen-carrying protein in the blood. The molecules break down and the atoms rearrange to form different molecules which dispose of the extra energy in the form of visible light photons. The process is called chemiluminescence.

CS investigators will spray a suspicious area, extinguish all light and see if a bluish-green light appears. If there are any blood traces in the area, they will glow. The main chemical in this reaction is luminol.

Luminol or C8H7O3N3, is a powdery compound made up of nitrogen, hydrogen, oxygen and carbon. You can make your own luminol spray by mixing luminol powder with a liquid containing hydrogen peroxide (H2O2) and hydroxide (OH-) and pouring the liquid into a spray bottle.

Sometimes CS investigators use other chemiluminescent chemicals, such as fluorescein, instead of luminol. These chemicals work the same basic way, but the procedure is a little bit different.

If luminol reveals traces of blood spatter, investigators will photograph or videotape the crime scene to record the pattern.

But the important thing to remember here is that luminol only indicates that there might be blood in an area. It may not be conclusive because other substances such as household bleach can also cause the luminol to glow. So, other tests should be run to ensure that the substance is actually human blood.

Experienced investigators can make a reliable identification based on how quickly the reaction occurs, but they still need to run other tests to verify that it is really human blood. Although Luminol may only reveal faint traces of blood it often leads investigators to search further for more blood. But despite what you might see on television CS investigators will only to spray luminol as a last resort simply because it tends to destroy other evidence.

They will also be looking for trace evidence, dried blood and prints. It is normal practice to take away towels, bedding, clothing, cloths, and couch covers. These are brought to the lab where technicians shake out the items in a sterile room, onto a large, white slab covered with paper.

BLOOD

If there is blood at the scene the chances are that the CS investigators will find it. One place in which they always look, though not usually at the actually crime scene, more often at the lab, is under the victim's nails.

If there was a struggle, and usually there is, there is a pretty good chance that traces of the offender's skin and therefore his DNA, will be under the victim's nails.

There may be dried blood on a piece of furniture or carpet. This will be sent to the lab. If the blood is on something which cannot be transported to a lab then the CS investigators will scrape the dried blood into a sterile container usually by using a scalpel.

Followers of the American crime show, *Dexter*, "everyone's favorite serial killer" will be aware of blood spatter analysis. Blood spatter, often incorrectly called "blood splatter," produce patterns. These patterns can actually reveal the exact type of weapon used in an attack. Common patterns would include a "cast-off pattern," a "low-velocity pattern" and a "high velocity pattern."

A "cast-off pattern" is left when a weapon such as a baseball bat contacts a blood source and then swings back. The blood droplets produced are large and often tear-drop shaped. A "cast-off pattern" indicates multiple blows from a blunt object, because the first blow typically does not contact any blood.

Another type of pattern is a "low-velocity pattern," usually the result of dripping blood. The force of impact is five feet per second or less. The size of the droplets is somewhere between four and eight millimeters. This type of blood spatter often occurs where, for example, the victim is stabbed and then walks around bleeding. The resulting drops are called passive spatters. Low-velocity spatters can also result from bleeding sustained from a punch.

Gunshot wounds usually produce high-velocity spatters but they can be caused by other weapons if the offender uses an extreme amount of force. The spatters travel more than 100 feet per second and usually look like a fine spray of tiny droplets. Bullet wounds are somewhat unique because they can have both back and front spatters, or just back spatters. This depends on whether the bullet lodged after entering the victim's body or traveled right through it. Usually, the back spatter is much smaller than the front spatter. This is because the blood spatter travels in the direction of the bullet.

HAIR AND FIBERS

Hair and fibers are collected from the crime scene by using a collection of combs, tweezers, containers and a filtered vacuum device. In case of rape and sexual assault the victim will be brought to a hospital where, during a medical examination, the body will be searched for hair and fibers. Anything found will be placed into sterile containers, sealed, logged and brought to the lab.

If there is a suspect then items of clothing including shoes will be examined for matching fibers. Forensic experts are able to use hair DNA to identify or eliminate suspects by comparison. The presence of hair or fibers on a tool or weapon can assist in identifying it as a weapon. Tests can be carried out on a single strand of hair which will determine not only what type of animal it came from, for example, human, dog, or cat but they will also be able to determine if it came from a human, the person's race, what part of the body it came from, whether it fell out or was pulled and whether it was dyed.

IMPRESSIONS

The three main types of impressions are fingerprints, footwear and tools. Fingerprints will be dealt with under a separate chapter because although they are lifted at the scene all analysis is carried out by forensic experts at the lab.

A footwear impression in mud or a tool mark on a window frame is an example of a three-dimensional impression. Where it is not feasible to submit the entire object containing the impression to the crime lab, the CS investigators will make a casting at the scene.

Usually a casting kit includes multiple casting compounds (dental gypsum, Silicone rubber), snow wax (for making a cast in snow), a bowl, a spatula and cardboard boxes to hold the casts.

Footwear impressions discovered in mud will first of all be photographed before a cast is made. To prepare the casting material, they will mix a casting material and water in a Ziploc-type bag and knead it for about two minutes, until the consistency is like pancake batter. They will then pour this mixture into the edge of the track so that it flows into the impression without causing air bubbles. Once the material overflows the impression, they let it set for about half an hour. Once set it is lifted carefully out of the mud.

The cast should not be cleaned or brushed as this might

destroy any trace evidence. The fully set cast is then placed into a cardboard box and brought to the lab for further analysis.

Tool mark impressions are much more difficult to cast. If it's not possible to remove the entire item containing the tool mark, a CS investigator can make a silicone-rubber cast. Usually there are two types of tool marks one might find at a crime scene; impressed or striated.

In the former a hard object contacts a softer object without moving back and forth. An example would be a hammer mark on a door frame. The tool mark is an impression of the hammer's shape. But it is difficult to make a definite match with an impressed tool mark.

In the latter, a hard object contacts a softer object and moves back and forth. An example would be pry marks (chips and scratches) on a window frame. The tool mark is a series of parallel lines. In this case it is easier to make a definite match with a striated tool mark.

In tool mark analysis, the forensic experts might be able to determine what sort of tool made the mark and whether a tool in evidence is the tool that made it. They may also be able to compare the tool mark in evidence to another tool mark to see if the marks were made by the same tool

THE CHAIN OF EVIDENCE

The chain of evidence is an important legal concept, which requires that the origin and history of any exhibit to be presented as evidence in a court of law must be clearly demonstrated to have followed an unbroken chain from its source to the court. If a defendant can prove that the chain was broken then there is a good likelihood that he will be acquitted.

All persons handling the sample, the places and conditions of storage must be documented with a note of the time, date, place and signature, where appropriate. This is the reason why, in processing the evidence, the fewer people handling the evidence the better. There is less likelihood of contamination and a shorter chain of custody to affect admissibility in court. In most countries, procedures relating to the chain of evidence are set out in a Code of Practice. In Britain, the manner in which police officers maintain the chain of evidence, that is, record, retain and reveal to the prosecutor, relevant material obtained during a criminal investigation is now dealt with by means of a *Code of Practice under the Criminal Procedure and Investigations Act 1996.*

6 FINGERPRINTS

"If someone hacks your password, you can change it - as many times as you want. You can't change your fingerprints. You have only ten of them. And you leave them on everything you touch; they are definitely not a secret. What's more, a password doesn't uniquely identify its owner, a fingerprint does. Let me put it this way: if hackers get a hold of your thumbprint, they could use it to identify and impersonate you for the rest of your life."
 Senator Al Franken *in a letter to Apple about his concerns about hacking on their fingerprint Ap*

The five protagonists in the evolution of fingerprints as a method of apprehending criminals are Sir William Herschel (1833-1917), Henry Faulds (1843-1930), Francis Galton (1822-1911), Juan Vucetich (1858-1925) and Sir Edward Richard Henry (1850–1931).

Herschel was the Chief Magistrate of the Hooghly district in Jungipoor, India when in 1858 he first began using fingerprints for the purposes of identifying parties to a legal contract. Instead of them signing the document he would take an imprint of their palm and affix it to the contract. Rajyadhar Konai, a local businessman, is credited as being the first person Herschel handprinted, apparently more as a way of getting him to honor a contract he had signed, rather than as a means of identification. He later used prints just of the right index and middle fingers. It was in this way that the first wide-scale, modern-day use of fingerprints was predicated.

Henry Faulds studied medicine, became a missionary and in 1873 was sent to Japan where he founded and then became the surgeon superintendent of Tuskiji Hospital in Tokyo. In the late 1870s, Henry Faulds became involved in archaeological digs in Japan and noticed on shards of ancient pottery the fingerprints of those who had made them. In 1880 Faulds published a paper in *Nature* magazine on fingerprints, observing that they could be used to catch criminals and suggesting how this could be done. Shortly after this Sir William Herschel, published a letter in *Nature,* stating that he had been using fingerprints in India as a method of signature on contracts.

When Faulds returned to Britain in 1886 Scotland Yard were offered and declined his fingerprint system. Faulds died in 1930 and it is recorded that he was bitter at the lack of recognition he had received for his work in forensic fingerprinting.

Although Francis Galton was not the first to propose the use of fingerprints for identification he was the first to place their study on a scientific basis, and so lay the groundwork for their use in criminal cases. His research laid the foundation for meaningful comparison of different prints. In 1892 he published his work in his book, *Finger Prints,* in which he proposed that all fingerprint patterns could be placed into one of three categories: loops, arches and whorls.

He was the first to assert the uniqueness of fingerprints and the fact that they did not change throughout life. He also provided the first workable fingerprint classification system. This system was later to be used by Edward Henry for practical use in police forces and other bureaucratic settings. In fact, it was Galton's extensive popular advocacy of the use of prints that convinced a somewhat skeptical public that they could be used reliably for identification.

In the realm of criminology it was the Argentine Juan Vucetich who in 1892 made the first criminal fingerprint identification. In the murder trial of Francis Rojas, a woman who murdered her two sons and cut her own throat in an attempt to place blame on another, Vucetich was able to prove she was the culprit by fingerprint evidence. He based his fingerprint classification system on that devised by Galton. But unlike Galton who used only the prints from the forefinger, Vucetich used the prints from all ten digits.

But the person who contributed most to the fingerprint system was Edward Richard Henry. Between 1903 and 1918 he was the Commissioner of Police of the Metropolis of London. He is responsible for developing the fingerprint identification system that is used throughout Europe and North America. In conjunction with his research, Henry published *Classification and Uses of Finger Prints*. As the head of Scotland Yard, he led the transition from anthropometry to fingerprint identification.

He was also one of the first scientists to study and report on the significance of bloodstains left at a crime scene and the man responsible for the introduction of police dogs.

The Henry fingerprint classification system rests on the principle that all fingerprints fall into one of four main types, Loops, Whorls, Arches and Compounds. This facilitates the categorization of ten-print fingerprint records into primary groupings based on fingerprint pattern types.

Primary classification combines arches with loops (L) and compounds with whorls (W). Both hands are viewed together and grouped into five pairs of fingers. The system assigns each finger a number according to the order in which is it located in the hand, beginning with the right thumb as number 1 and ending with the little finger of the left hand as number 10.

The system also assigns a numerical value to fingers that contain a whorl pattern; fingers 1 and 2 each have a value of 16, fingers 3 and 4 have a value of 8, and so on, with the final two fingers having a value of 1. Fingers with a non-whorl pattern, such as an arch or loop pattern, have a zero value.

All of the ridges of fingerprints form patterns called loops, whorls or arches. Loops, of which there are two types, start on one side of the finger, curve around or upward, and exit the other side. Whorls form a circular or spiral pattern while arches slope upward and then down.

PRINTS AT THE SCENE OF A CRIME

Everyone's hands and feet are naturally oily. This is due to the eccrine glands, which secrete sweat, a mixture of water, salts, and other trace compounds. The sweat will stick to the friction ridges of the finger. So, when a finger is placed on a surface such as glass, plastic, or wood, an impression known as a fingerprint will be left behind. The natural oils of the body will preserve the fingerprint.

Fingerprints are absolutely distinct in that, it is believed that, no two people have the same fingerprints. In fact, they are even more unique than DNA. Identical twins can share the same DNA, or at least most of it, but they cannot share the same fingerprints.

Latent fingerprints are made from substances other than sweat such as blood, other body fluids, or paint. Part of the analysis performed on latent fingerprints includes a determination of what the fingerprint was made from, as this may provide additional evidence about the criminal or the crime.

One of the first matters CS investigators attend to when they arrive at a crime scene, after photographing it, is to dust for latent fingerprints. Dusting for fingerprints ensures that no prints are missed, even if patent fingerprints, those readily visible to the naked eye, are evident. The CS investigator will gently brush specialized fingerprint powder over various surfaces to see if any appear. If latent fingerprints appear, they are first of all photographed and then carefully lifted with clear tape before being affixed to fingerprint cards.

A process known as fuming may be used to find latent fingerprints on difficult surfaces. Fuming may also be used for very old fingerprints, because it causes a chemical reaction with trace substances which may be left behind by a fingerprint, even if the sweat itself has gone. Because the image that appears is only temporary it should be photographed immediately.

Powder will not reveal all latent prints because there are some surfaces that powder will not adhere to, such as the human skin. Often in crime programs you will see a criminal wiping away his prints with a cloth. This does not wipe away a print. To wipe away a print completely you need to use a very strong bleach.

CS investigators now use two other chemicals in sprays to obtain fingerprints, Cyanoacrylate and Ninhydrin. Cyanoacrylate is also used in superglue. In addition to being sticky it also reacts with human sweat to make it white. It is the spray used to show up prints on human skin.

Ninhydrin reacts with human sweat to make it purple and can be used on surfaces such as wallpaper. Both sprays are usually used with a special ultra violet (UV) light source which makes it easier to view the patterns in the latent prints.

In 1976 Xerox Research Centre of Canada discovered a

method for the detection of latent fingerprints by their inherent luminescence using continuous-wave (CW) argon-ion laser excitation. Essentially, the laser procedure involves illumination of the exhibit under scrutiny with the blue-green light from the argon-ion laser and photography of the resulting yellow-green fingerprint luminescence.

Both the viewing and photography are carried out in a dark room. A filter is used to block the laser light scattered from the exhibit to prevent eye damage and film exposure by the laser light.

LIFTING PRINTS

Lifting prints either from a living or dead person usually involves the same procedure. The fingers are rolled on an ink pad from cuticle to cuticle and prints taken from each finger are deposited onto a ten print card with numbered boxes, starting with the right thumb and proceeding to the little finger in the top row. The process is repeated with the left hand for the bottom row of the card, starting with the left thumb and ending with the little finger of the left hand.

To identify a particular person from their fingerprints, a complete set of inked fingerprints is taken and sent to the IDENT1 database. Although most law enforcement agencies employ some in-house forensic scientists it is more common to buy in forensic science services from a private company, as and when required. However, fingerprinting is an exception simply because it pre-dates the development of many of the techniques now in use. Fingerprinting is generally an in-house function and fingerprints are shared on the IDENTI database.

In Britain everyone arrested for a recordable offence has their fingerprints, palm prints and limited nominal data taken and entered onto the database. DNA and mug-shot photographs are also obtained. NPIA is responsible for the National Fingerprint Database (IDENT1), providing the Police service in England, Scotland and Wales with a fingerprint identification system. Although it is a centralized search and record system, the operational use of IDENT1 is devolved to the police service, where it is accessed and used each of the 51 fingerprint bureaus of England, Scotland and Wales, on a 24 hour basis. The technology includes an Automated Fingerprint Identification System (AFIS) search engine and two principal databases, one contains the national fingerprint (ten print) database with over eight million identity records and a second holding unidentified crime scene marks. American states also share fingerprint databases.

Dactyloscopy is the technical name used for the comparison of fingerprints. Comparison rules vary from country to country. In Britain there must be sixteen points of comparison from the print under analysis to that of the suspect. But in Australia and New Zealand only eight points of congruence are required. In the United States there is no longer a fixed number of comparison points.

RIDGES AND THE COMPANISON PROCESS

For comparison purposes, a fingerprint consists of the friction ridge skin of the end joint of each finger taken from cuticle to cuticle. Fingerprints are attributable to the tiny ridges, whorls and valley patterns on the tip of each finger. There are six major types of ridges:

Bifurcations: ridges that split into two.
Ending ridge: a simple straight ridge.
Dot or island: tiny round ridges.
Short ridge: small, isolated segment of ridge.
Enclosure or anastomosis: a ridge that forks and forms a

complete circle and then becomes a single ridge again. Trifurcation: a ridge that splits into three.

Taken together the ridge characteristics of a fingerprint are known as its minutiae. It is the types and location of the minutiae that give the uniqueness to a fingerprint. A fingerprint expert will usually begin by studying the prints as a whole and then proceed to making a comparison between equivalent parts of the prints to see if they match. Once he is satisfied that there is a match, he will draw up a list of the matching points before completing his report.

Even where tips of the fingers have been damaged as a result of mummification, decomposition or excessive wetting, a fingerprint expert has special techniques available which he can use. So the fact that a body has been dumped in a lake does not necessarily mean that its fingerprints will have been destroyed. There are basically three types of prints which can be found at a crime scene, Visible, Molded and Latent. Visible prints are left by the transfer of blood, paint or another fluid or powder onto a surface that is smooth enough to hold the print; evident to the naked eye. Molded prints are usually found in a soft medium like soap, putty or candle wax. Latent prints are left by the transfer of sweat and natural oils from the fingers onto a surface that is smooth enough to hold the print; not visible to the naked eye

Two inaccuracies consistently appear on TV programs relating to prints. When you see a detective using a handkerchief to turn the handle of a door knob he's not actually protecting a print, he's destroying it. Also, you've probably seen police in *Dexter* scanning a print into a computer and waiting a few moments for it to spit out a photo of the suspect. The reality is that the software will return several possible matches that an expert then analyzes visually to determine a definite match.

7 FIREARMS AND BALLISTICS

"You can get much farther with a kind word and a gun, than you can with a kind word alone."
Al Capone, *American Gangster*

Ballistics refers to the science of the travel of a projectile in flight. It is the area of forensic science that deals with firearms, how they are used, why they are used and why they are used frequently in the commission of crime.

Most firearms have their own unique identifying features. So even if an offender takes the gun with him from the scene of a crime a good ballistics expert can derive a substantial amount of information from the bullet, the nature of the wound and any residue that is left around it. If the firearm has been left at the scene of the crime, the weapon itself can go a long way to providing valuable information about the person who has committed the offence.

That is why a professional hitman will take the gun and the bullet with him.

There are various different types of firearms. Pistols are small firearms usually used by police and other security personnel and serve mainly as a defensive weapon of last resort. They are commonly used in violent crime because of their compact size, low cost, and ease of operation making them a common weapon in violent crime.

The two classes of pistol are revolvers and automatics. Revolvers are pistols that contain a revolving cylinder with chambers that hold individual cartridges. As the weapon is cocked, the next chamber comes into line with the firing pin and barrel. After the gun is fired the cartridge remains in the cylinder and must be manually removed.

Automatics, on the other hand, contain a mechanism which is actuated by the energy of recoil. It feeds cartridges from a magazine in the grip which are ejected from the pistol automatically.

A rifle is a long firearm designed to be fired from the shoulder. There are numerous types of rifles including single shot, semi-automatic and automatic. Together with shotguns, these are often called "long guns."

These weapons can be further classified according to their rifling. A Steyr has four grooves. The grooves and lands are of equal width with a right hand twist. A Browning has six grooves, narrow lands, broad grooves with a right hand twist. Colts have six grooves, narrow lands, broad grooves and a left hand twist. A Webley has seven grooves, narrow lands, broad grooves and a right hand twist. A Smith and Wesson has five grooves and the grooves and lands are of equal width with a right hand twist.

Machine guns are automatic weapons capable of rapid, sustained fire and are classified into three groups; the squad automatic, the general purpose machine gun and the heavy machine gun. The squad automatic weapon is chambered for small-caliber assault-rifle ammunition and designed to be operated by one person. The general-purpose machine gun, firing full-power rifle ammunition, is designed for operation by two persons while the heavy machine gun fires rounds of 12.7 mm (.5 in) or higher. These weapons have heavy recoil and cannot be safely fired even when held with two hands. They are designed to be fired using a stabilizing bi-pod or fixed mounting.

Sub machine guns are lightweight automatic small-arms chambered for relatively low-energy pistol cartridges and fired from the hip or shoulder. They usually hold 10–50 cartridges and are rarely effective at more than 200 yards.

They can fire 650 or more rounds per minute and weigh between 6–10lbs. Examples would include a Thompson, a Sten and the Israeli Uzi.

Finally, shotguns are light, smooth-bored gun which often have double-barrels. They are especially designed for firing small shot at short range. Criminals often adapt shotguns by illegally sawing off a large part of the barrel.

BALLISTIC EVIDENCE AT A CRIME SCENE

Any ballistic evidence collected at a crime scene will be logged and bagged and sent to the lab for forensic analysis. Usually, the evidence sent for analysis would include the actual firearm itself, spent bullets, spent cartridge cases, spent shot shells and/or shot, shot shell wadding, live ammunition and clothing.

The role of a forensic ballistic expert is to examine certain characteristics of firearms that relate to the bullets fired from them, including the caliber of the firearm and the rifling pattern contained in the barrel of the firearm. If a CS investigator finds a firearm at the scene of a crime he will not pick it up by inserting a pen inside the barrel as this will almost certainly leave its own mark on the lands of the rifling. The correct way for a crime scene investigator to handle the weapon is by wearing gloves and placing it in a bag for subsequent examination.

THE DUTIES OF A BALLISTIC EXPERT

The main duties of a ballistic expert are to identify the firearm, compare ammunition, determine the distance and angle of trajectory, endeavor to restore a serial number, if erased, and identify trace evidence.

The important thing to remember about firearms and

bullets is that the slight variations in bullets fired from two different guns are immediately apparent to the ballistics expert. A ballistic expert can determine that a bullet has been fired from a particular weapon because of the process of barrel manufacture. When it is first made the barrel is smooth bored and then reamed to a specific diameter before being rifled. The tools used to make the barrels are eroded slightly with each gun that is made. The result is that it is impossible to produce two identical gun barrels. Bullets fired from different guns will always have different striation marks.

The significance of this is that just like fingerprints, no two firearms, even if they are of the same make and model, will produce the same marks on fired bullets and cartridge cases. Furthermore, it is not simply the processes involved in the manufacture but the actual use of the firearm which leaves surface characteristics that cannot be exactly reproduced in any other firearm.

Normally, the firearm itself does not change very much over a period of time. So firearms which are recovered months or even years after a shooting can be identified by forensic experts as having fired a specific bullet or cartridge case.

FILING OFF SERIAL NUMBERS

Many criminal believe, again from crime television programs, that firearms that have had their serial numbers filed off cannot be identified. Well, as the song goes, it ain't necessarily so. Ballistic experts have several methods they use to reveal the serial number no matter how much of the number has been destroyed. This is because whenever metal is pressure stamped, not only does the metal have indentations of numbers, but the metal underneath the numbers contains resultant structural abnormalities. In order to reveal those numbers experts will use one of three methods; the magnaflux method, the chemical and electrochemical etching method, and the ultrasonic cavitation method.

In the magnaflux method the firearm is first magnetized. This produces ripples of magnetic forces used to locate where the metal is disordered from the pressure stamping process. Then the firearm is sprayed with an oil that suspends any iron-like particles. These particles will settle in places where the metal is disordered. This reveals the location of the hidden serial number. This is probably the best method because it is not destructive and does not change the weapon in any way.

The second method is the chemical and electrochemical etching method where the expert paints what is known as an etching solution over the area in question. The solution etches the disordered metal more quickly than the sound metal around it. The result is that the missing numbers should immediately come into view. If you apply an electrical current which is an electrochemical etching, the process is speeded up. The only problem with this method is that it changes the physical make-up of the evidence.

The third method they used is called the ultrasonic cavitation method which is not used so often due to its destructive nature. In this method the firearm is placed in a special ultrasonic bath and inundated it with super high frequency vibrations. These bring about the cavitation which is the process whereby tiny bubbles are produced along the surface of the metal. With repeated exposure, the process of cavitation starts eating away at the metal thus revealing the serial number. So, a firearm which has had its serial number erased does not necessarily mean it cannot be identified by a forensic ballistics expert.

AMMUNITION COMPARISON

A ballistic expert will examine cartridges and cartridge cases for similarities in breech marks, elector marks, firing pin impressions, extractor marks, and other named toolmarks. The firing pin of a firearm leaves exactly the same markings on every bullet that it expels. Therefore, even when bullets are so damaged that there is no point in analyzing them, the striation marks which are the marks left by the firing pin, are still available for comparison. A ballistic expert will fire off a round using the suspect gun and subsequently compare the bullet and case fired with the bullet and case collected from the scene of the crime. If the markings match then they know it was fired from the same gun.

IDENTIFICATION OF TRACE EVIDENCE

If you fire a gun or even hold one that has been fired the chances are that firearms discharge residue will attach to your clothes and hands. This is because when the trigger is pulled and the firing pin strikes the bullet, the primer in the back of the bullet will react with the propellant and cause a small explosion. It will also create gases which escape from a hole in the top of the gun. This is what is referred to as gunshot residue.

But even guns themselves can leave residue on you if you come into contact with them because of the oil used to lubricate the working parts. If a suspect is present at the crime scene his hand will usually be wiped with a treated swab. If residues are present a special dye on the swab will turn purple. However, all this will tell the police is that a firearm has been used. It cannot indicate which gun was used. Neither does it, by itself, prove that the person who handled the gun was the person who committed the crime by pulling the trigger.

THE TRAJECTORY

A medical person may examine the blackening of the skin around the entry wound of a victim to determine the angle at which a bullet entered the body if he believes that such information may have evidential value. If the blackening to the skin is more intense above the wound, this would indicate that the weapon was held at an upward angle.

GUNSHOT WOUNDS

It's normal for the ballistic expert to collaborate with the forensic pathologist in matters relating to gunshot wounds. In contact wounds where the gun is held against the body, the skin around the entry wound is blackened and may be pinkish in color due to the emission of carbon monoxide. The entry hole of the bullet will usually have a splintered or star shaped appearance. This is because when a bullet leaves the barrel of the weapon it exhibits a degree of wobble or tail wag before it stabilizes.

It is this tail wag that actually tears the skin and produces this ragged-edge effect. Even a shot that is fired from as little as a meter away will produce this effect, but to a less significant extent. If fired from a greater distance there will be little or no blackening of the entry hole.

Provided that the bullet is not deflected by bones, in its passage through the body, the exit wound should be a similar size. In the event that the bullet does strike bone then the resultant distortion of the bullet and any bone material it carries with it will create a much bigger exit wound. All firearms, bullets or casings at the scene will be picked up by a CS investigator (wearing gloves) bagged and logged.

When there are bullet holes in the victim or in other

objects at the scene, ballistic experts can determine where and from what height the bullet was fired, as well as the position of the victim when it was fired, simply by using a laser trajectory kit. In cases where bullets are embedded in a wall or door frame, the CS investigator will cut out the portion of the wall or frame containing the bullet. But hey will definitely not dig the bullet out with a penknife as often seen on television as this can so damage the bullet as to render it unsuitable for comparison purposes.

8 DOCUMENTS AND COMPUTERS

"You know something is wrong when the government declares opening someone else's mail is a felony but your internet activity is fair game for data collecting."
E. A. Bucchianeri, *We Are Warned.*

It is normal for a CS investigator to collect and take away any documentation they consider relevant to a crime. These may include diaries, planners, phone books, suicide notes, signed contracts, receipts, torn up letters, the contents of a trash can or, in fact, any other written, typed or photocopied evidence that might be related to the crime. It is amazing what can now be recovered by forensic experts from documents you think might have been destroyed or damaged beyond repair.

Later on we will show you how a forensic expert can often reconstruct a destroyed document, even one that has been burned, as well as determine if a document has been altered. Technicians analyze documents for forgery, determine handwriting matches to the victim and suspects, and identify what type of machine was used to produce the document. They can rule out a printer or photocopier found at the scene or determine compatibility or incompatibility with a machine found in a suspect's possession.

CS investigators will also remove computers, hard drives, personal laptops, mobile phone and other apparatus than can record any information on it. Even information which has been deleted from a computer can be re-produced. This will be dealt with in a separate chapter called Cyber Crime. No such documentation nor any computers should be removed unless there is a proper warrant authorizing their removal. If the warrants are, in any way, faulty any evidence acquired will be inadmissible.

9 CAUSE OF DEATH – THE AUTOPSY

Lawyer: "Doctor, before you performed the autopsy, did you check for a pulse?"
Doctor Witness: "No."
Lawyer: "Did you check for blood pressure?"
Doctor: "No."
Lawyer: "Did you check for breathing?"
Doctor: "No."
Lawyer: "So, then it is possible that the patient was alive when you began the autopsy?"
Doctor: "No."
Lawyer: "How can you be so sure, Doctor?"
Doctor: "Because his brain was sitting on my desk in a jar."
Lawyer: "But could the patient have still been alive nevertheless?"
Doctor: "Yes, it is possible that he could have been alive and practicing law somewhere."
Transcript *of Actual American Murder Trial*

In the event that a crime scene contains a dead body then a forensic pathologist will usually be summoned to attend if the death is suspicious. Such a visit will assist him to begin building a background to the case, and to take any samples required before the body is moved and an autopsy is carried out on the corpse. An autopsy is another name for a post-mortem. It is normal for the investigating officers and the pathologist to discuss the known facts of the case at the crime scene.

Once a body has been discovered the likelihood is that it will remain at the scene for several hours before it is moved. This is to preserve the scene and protect what might later prove to be valuable evidence. If the body is discovered late at night then a decision may be made to wait until the following morning to make a proper initial examination of the body and the scene.

The pathologist will be particularly interested in the position of the body and any body parts, tissue or blood, which may have become detached. The distance of these items from the body, their shape, trajectory and direction of their separation are all of great importance in determining what has happened. Before the pathologist arrives there will be extensive photographic coverage of the scene with the body *in situ*. This will be supported by meticulously accurate scale plans of the scene, diagrams of the body and any seemingly relevant articles.

The pathologist will take the temperature of the body and checks the ambient temperature of the location. This will assist him in calculating the time of death. When the pathologist has carried out his preliminary examination plastic or paper bags are placed over the hands and head of the body to prevent loss of any trace evidence and the body is wrapped in a plastic or paper sheet and placed in a body bag.

An autopsy or post-mortem is a surgical procedure consisting of a detailed examination of a corpse by a pathologist to determine the cause and manner of death, to evaluate any disease or injury which may be present, and to decide whether any medical diagnosis and treatment prior to death was appropriate. The word derives from the ancient Greek word *autopsia*, "to see for oneself", derived from autos "oneself" and opsis "view."

There are four types of autopsies:

Medico-legal, forensic or coroner autopsies;
Clinical or Pathological autopsies;
Anatomical or academic autopsies, and
Virtual or medical imaging autopsies.

We are concerned with the medico-legal type which seeks

to find the cause and manner of death and to identify the decedent. It is carried out, as prescribed by applicable law, where the death has been caused in a violent or suspicious manner, or has been sudden, or without medical assistance or during surgical procedures.

It is usually called a forensic autopsy and is undertaken primarily to ascertain the cause of death. In American law, deaths are classified under one of five manners: natural, accident, suicide, homicide and undetermined. Pathologists will also try to ascertain the time of death, and what, if anything, preceded the death, such as a struggle or altercation.

The examination may include taking biological specimens from the corpse for toxicological testing like stomach contents. These tests may indicate the presence of poison. Most American states require the pathologist to complete an autopsy report and many insist on the examination being videoed.

In Britain, forensic pathology is a service provided to the Coroners and Police Authorities to assist in the investigation of violent or suspicious deaths and forensic pathologists work within regional group practices which are independent of the Police Service, NPIA and the Home Office. Forensic pathologists can also be self-employed or employed in a number of different organizations including university departments. In England and Wales, forensic pathologists are accredited by the Home Office but in Scotland which has a different legal system, they operate under the Procurator Fiscal system.

The procedures carried out in an autopsy are, for the most part, all the same irrespective of the jurisdiction and will involve an external and internal examination.

EXTERNAL EXAMINATION

The person responsible for handling, cleaning and moving the body may be called a *diener* which is the German word for a servant or in the United Kingdom they are called an anatomical pathology technologist. On its arrival at the mortuary or medical examiner's office the body is weighed and measured. The *diener* will examine the plastic or paper sheet and body bag before any inspection of the body takes place. The sheet and bag are there to retain any articles that may have dropped out of the body en route to the mortuary.

Any objects found on the body, the sheet or in the body bag are bagged, sealed, marked with identification labels and logged. He will also remove the bags on the hands and feet and examine them. Next, samples of plucked and combed hair including the root are taken which can be used for DNA and drug analysis. He will take cuttings and scrapings from beneath each of the body's fingernails as they may contain dried blood, skin, fibers or other evidential material from the assailant.

Before the clothes are taken off he will carefully examine the cadaver for signs of foreign bodies, such as paint, pieces of wood, glass, dust, soil, oil or anything else that might have evidential value. Everything found is bagged, sealed, labelled and logged. Usually a photographic and/or video and sound recording will be made throughout the entire post-mortem procedure.

Clothing will be carefully removed, layer by layer, with careful examination and each item stored in plastic bags. Once again, everything is carefully labelled and recorded. Any damp articles are removed from the body and air dried before being packed. This will prevent shrinkage, which can alter relationships between holes and wounds.

Where the victim has been strangled with a ligature, the position of the knot is noted and photographed before the ligature is cut off some inches from the knot, thereby preserving it for later investigation. The examiner will look for any holes, marks, discolorations, scrapes and tears in the material of the clothing for later comparison with any wounds on the body.

Once all the clothing has been removed the naked body is then given a thorough examination. The *diener* will take further hair samples from the eye brows and pubic area, and samples are taken of any materials exuded from the body during or after death. In cases of asphyxia, such as drowning, bloodstained froth may appear around the nostrils and mouth.

The body will also be checked for any evidence of sexual interference so vaginal and rectal swabs will be taken to check for the possible presence of semen. In female victims, injury to the perineum may indicate rape, and in both male and female victims, damage to the anus could be indicative of penetration. Swabs are also taken from the mouth. There will be a careful examination of the conjunctivae to see if there are any blood spots caused by hemorrhaging in cases of asphyxia, or color changes attributable to the inhalation of carbon monoxide. The entire body is examined, inch by inch, for injuries, bruises, scars and marks caused by injections. If there are head injuries the surrounding hair will be shaved.

Wounds will be carefully measured, both in their extent and depth and also in relation to a fixed point on the body. Areas of wounds and injuries are usually plotted on to a pre-printed diagram of the human body along with details and measurements. The examiner might take further body temperature readings and note the extent of *rigor mortis* and body staining, due to the natural process of putrefaction.

This is to try and establish an accurate time of death. The body is then turned over so that the back of the body can be examined.

INTERNAL EXAMINATION

The *diener* will clean the body of dirt and blood and usually carry out an X-ray of the body. The pathologist is then ready to dissect. The *diener* or pathologist will place a plastic or rubber brick called a "body block" under the back of the body. This will cause the body's arms and neck to fall backwards while stretching and pushing the chest upwards to facilitate cutting with maximum exposure.

The reason for the dissection is to study the internal organs to see how external injuries connect to internal injuries. An example would be the study of bruising of the brain following a head injury, or damage to the heart and blood vessels following a stabbing or shooting. They will also look for evidence of disease as a cause of death, for example, heart attack, stroke, aneurysm or infection.

The stomach contents are important because they may provide clues to the time, circumstances or cause of death. The pathologist is now ready to make the cut. He can do this in several ways. He can make a large deep Y-shaped incision starting at the top of each shoulder and running down the front of the chest to the lowest part of the sternum. This is the most common approach. He could make a T-shaped incision from the tip of both shoulders, in a horizontal line across the region of the collar bones to meet at the sternum in the middle. Or, he could make a single vertical cut from the middle of the neck, near the "Adam's apple on a male victim." In each of these approaches the cut will extend all the way down to the pubic bone while making a deviation to the left side of the navel.

The Y-cut is the most popular as it opens up the breastplate and allows access to all the major organs including the heart, lungs, liver, stomach, and spleen. The incision begins with cuts behind each ear at an approximate angle of forty five degrees and along the neck, meeting at the top of the chest, then downwards in a straight line over the abdomen to the pubis.

In the United States pathologists prefer to make the initial incision on a horizontal line across the top of the shoulders as it is less disfiguring of the corpse. But the Y-cut allows a much better display of the larynx and makes the procedure of pulling back the skin of the face over the skull far less complicated, making it easier to demonstrate jaw fractures and other facial injuries.

After the Y-cut all major organs are removed and weighed. This is done because certain types of illness can cause a reduction or increase in the weight of organs such as the heart and the lungs. The organs can be removed in one unit but sometimes, depending on trauma to the body, they may be removed individually in a specific sequence.

After this the abdomen is examined and tissue samples taken for analysis and the contents of the stomach are examined to determine the last meal. Time frames can be established because as with anything we eat, the body takes time to digest it, removing valuable nutrients and energy producing elements and this takes time moving through the digestive tract. So we will have partially digested, completely digested and undigested food facilitating accurate estimates of the time of death.

The pathologist will also take samples of bile from the gall bladder, ocular (eye) fluid, liver tissue and urine for toxicology testing. This is because some poisons may not show in one part of the body but will show in others.

After this, the pathologist will concentrate on the head injuries. Sometimes, if head trauma is not visible on an external examination he will make a triangular incision across the top of the scalp to reveal the brain and first of all examines it inside the head. When finished he will remove the brain for a more thorough inspection and to take tissue samples.

SAMPLE COLLECTION

One of the primary aims of the pathologist conducting the autopsy is to collect as many samples as possible even though not all will be needed. He will extract a minimum of 20ml of clean blood which will be stored in a sterile container. Blood taken to determine alcohol levels is usually stored in bottles containing sodium fluoride as this inhibits further production of alcohol due to breakdown of sugar and bacterial action.

As well as determining the blood type the pathologist will be testing the blood for alcohol, glucose, carbon monoxide, carbon dioxide and other poisons. He will also take a urine sample to test for alcohol, metallic poisons, barbiturates, opiates, amphetamines, and other drugs. Urine is extracted by the use of a ladle or a pipette through an incision in the dome of the bladder.

Cerebro-spinal fluid will also be collected by lumbar puncture before dissection begins. This is usually extracted with the needle of a syringe inserted between two vertebrae of the spinal column with the body in a sitting, head between the knees position. Although it can be taken straight from the brain with a long needled syringe.

As well as examining the stomach contents he will also look at the contents of the intestines, preserving the small intestine for laboratory analysis. In cases where for example metallic poisoning is considered the large intestine will be preserved separately. The entire liver will be removed and examined for toxins. He will note the total weight of the liver and record it so as to enable calculation of the total amount of poison present.

The vitreous humor is the jelly like fluid found behind the lens of the eye. He will extract a sample by means of a fine needled syringe while later injecting an equal amount of water back into the eye to prevent its collapse. The vitreous humor can provide an accurate indication of the time of death.

When all of these procedures have been carried out and the test performed the contents will be returned to the cadaver and the body will be sown back up. The autopsy report will be furnished to the coroner and its finding given to the police investigating team. The samples are given to the CD investigators. They assume responsibility for their proper labelling and custody. Where the body is badly decomposed other specialists conduct examinations which we will deal with in the chapter entitled Identifying Decaying Bodies.

10 IDENTIFYING SKELETONS

"They say that even of a good thing you can have too much. But I doubt it. True, such good things as sunbathing, beer, and tobacco may be intemperately pursued to the detriment of their devotees; yet, to my mind, one cannot have too much of a good murder."
William Roughead, *Classic Crimes*

Obviously, the identification of a body is crucial to any criminal investigation but what happens when the body is so badly decomposed that a visual inspection will not prove identity? In such circumstances the police will call upon the services of a Forensic Anthropology with extensive anatomical and osteological training to analyze the remains.

When a corpse is left undiscovered for a long time, the soft tissues and organs may have disintegrated and all that will be left are skeletal remains. In such case the pathologist will need specialist help in the form of a forensic anthropologist. After identifying them as human bones, his first role will be to assemble the bones in anatomical order. He will then know what bones are missing and whether the bones consist of one or more bodies. Whilst it is highly unlikely that a complete animal skeleton would be mistaken for that of a human, small bones, such as isolated bones from the paws of bears, can cause confusion.

Having determined that the bones are human he will then seek to identify the gender, approximate age, physical stature, and likely racial affiliation of the person in life. The examination can also indicate the approximate time since death, likely cause of death and any identifying illnesses or wounds suffered in life that could leave traces in the bone structure. This information is then used to assist in the identification of the body. An examination of the skeletal remains will focus on two main areas: Osteology, the examination of bones and Dentition, the examination of the teeth.

OSTEOLOGY

Despite the fact that after death they may have been burned, immersed in water or attacked by corrosive maters, bones can be durable enough to provide sufficient information to enable forensic anthropologists to identify to whom they belong.

As human grown from babies to teenagers a process known as "ossification" occurs where their bones become stronger and thicker and finally fuse together. Ossification is the best guide to revealing the age of a child's skeleton as it occurs in 800 points of the body. For example, when a child reaches the age of six, the two bone plates form at either end of the outer forearm. By the age of seventeen in males and twenty in females, the lower bone plate and the radius fuse together. Shortly afterwards the upper bone plate and radius also fuse together. The collarbone is the last bone in the body to finish growing, usually when people reach twenty-eight.

As people grow older degeneration in their bones will commence. Anthropologists will look for tiny spikes that start to appear on the edges of the vertebrae, signs of arthritis and the wearing of teeth due to age. All of our bones deteriorate with age.

In order to determine the gender of a skeleton anthropologists examine the skull and the pelvic bones. The human skull will provide the most information and the three areas they look at are the ridges located above the eyes, the bone situated just below the ear and the occiput.

The occiput is the bone which is located at the lower back of the skull. The difference in the pelvis is more obvious. The male pelvis tends to be narrow and flat, whereas in the female the pelvis is wider and bowl shaped, being built for child bearing.

In addition to the skull and pelvic bones anthropologists will also rely on some smaller differences in other bones.

They can determine the height by reassembling the skeleton and measuring the length of significant bones. The addition of 10-11cm or four inches onto the bone length will account for the missing tissue and muscle and provide an accurate estimation of the deceased's original height. But if parts of the skeleton are missing, certain individual bones, such as the femur, will be used as a height guide. The femur is the first bone to be measured because the longer the bone is, the better and more accurate the estimate will be. The height of a human is usually gauged at two and two thirds the length of the femur. However, other factors to be considered are the race and sex of the skeleton.

Bones will also reveal such matters as birth defects, diseases, and injuries. Bones can be damaged by birth defects like spina-bifida, cancer, poor diet and some infectious diseases. In the case of injuries, broken bones and mended bones are easily visible and because they are so easily visible, mended bones can reveal identity.

The skeletal remains of a victim who died violently will be evident in the bones. For example, a bullet wound will leave a round hole. Sometimes even the bullet will still be trapped which can then be traced back to the original weapon. Bones may even disclose the path of a bullet through the body. Bones may be damaged or cut with sharp weapons, such as knives, axes or blades, or even crushed by blunt force trauma, as in a beating or a high speed collision.

Although distinguishing between fractures that occurred pre- and post–mortem can present difficulties there are certain indications an anthropologist may observe which will help him, like, for example, the bones of a deceased person break differently compared to the bones of a living person. Healing at the edge of a fracture indicates that injuries occurred during life.

DENTITION

Just like bones, teeth and even dentures are also very durable and can greatly assist in identifying bodies. Human teeth are quite distinctive and accordingly are easier to recognize than animal teeth. The foods that most humans eat is processed or soft food which does not require substantial chewing or tearing. The age of the skeleton can be identified solely by reference to its teeth. Before we reach eighteen we will still have some of our milk teeth and it is around this time that wisdom teeth first appear.

FACIAL RECONSTRUCTION

When skeletal remains are found, and the victim remains unidentified after traditional means of identification fail, investigators may call upon the forensic artist to utilize the three-dimensional facial reconstruction technique. This is a technique that produces an actual three dimensional model of the head and face of the skull. Whilst the application of the technique requires great skill and experience, based upon strict adherence to scientific fact and the possession of great artistic flair, it is actually based upon a disarmingly simple idea. Several different techniques are used. The British technique involves using clay, modelling tools and a packet of cocktail sticks. The process starts with the production of a cast of the skull using Algenate compound. The empty eye sockets of the cast are filled with polystyrene eyeballs and the gaps around them filled in. The sculptor then drills tiny holes at anatomically significant points in the skull, pushing pieces of cocktail stick, the tissue markers, to a predetermined depth read from a table which shows the estimated thickness of body tissue at that point.

The musculature is gradually built up over the face with modelling clay to the height of the pegs. First the jaw and neck are constructed, followed by the cheeks and temples, then the mouth and the eyes are added. The type of nose can prove difficult. This is because the skull provides the barest of information. It is in this particular area that the artistic skill and interpretation of the sculptor is so important.

The sculptor then fills out the muscles of the cheeks and jaw and applies thin strips of clay to the forehead and scalp to represent thin layers of tissue. Once the skull has been covered in clay, the surface is smoothed out to represent skin. The accuracy of ears and facial hair are also dependent on the skill and experience of the artist. Hair is accomplished either by means of a wig, or by applying clay to represent hair.

Various items like Theatrical props, such as glasses, clothing, hats, etc. may be applied to better accentuate the features of the individual. When the sculpture is finished it is photographed. All procedures are documented and working notes collected. When executed properly, this technique can produce a very high success rate.

Information such as geographic location of where the deceased lived, his or her lifestyle, and the various information provided to the artist by the forensic anthropologist and other professionals, is heavily relied upon when completing the reconstruction.

VIDEO SUPERIMPOSITION

A developing technique of human identification is video superimposition, a scientific advance on the photographic imposition which was used for the first time in 1935 in the Ruxton murder case. Video superimposition uses the same techniques as photographic superimposition, but makes use of the ability of computers to manipulate the image.

COMPUTER-ASSISTED FACIAL RECONSTRUCTION

Revolutionary computer software now allows computer facial reconstruction, a virtual form of reconstructing the face from a skull. This makes it easy and efficient to travel from computer to computer. The software provides a 3D image/structure of the finished face to be rotated and moved around on a monitor.

While computer facial reconstruction does not require artistic skill, it does require skills of a different kind. There is no standard method of computer facial reconstruction but the initial data and facial shape comes from a 3D scan of the skull. This process is non-destructive to the skull and involves the skull rotating on a turning table whilst a laser scanner lights up a thin perpendicular strip.

Mirrors located on either side of the turning table reflect the images from the lit area to sensors. The data that the scan produces allows a controlling program to identify the distances of each point located on the skull. This provides a digitalized model of the skull that is easily and freely rotated on the computer screen.

CT - COMUTER TOMOGRAPHY

Applying muscle and skin to the bone requires computer tomography, (CT) scans of actual living people, which acquire images showing where bones cast shadows onto the skull and record hard and soft tissue, indicating bones and flesh in a 3 dimensional view. Using CT scans, data files record the shape of the skull as well as the tissue depth. Forensic anthropologists' knowledge is also utilized in choosing an appropriate form of CT scan.

Any clothing found with the bones can provide a clothing size, which is useful, as it allows scientists to adjust any tissue depth measurements to account for obesity or thinness. Merging the two scans, the CT scan is applied to the digital scan of the skull, becoming two skulls on top of each other. At this stage of the process, the two skulls are different shapes. The computer program distorts the skulls' marks on both so they match each other and at the same time, distorting the facial tissue properties, creating a facial shape that resembles the victim.

COLOR MAPPING

The problem with CT scans is that they cannot record vital details like hair, skin and eye color. These aspects must be added by borrowing the physical features of a living person in order to paint these features onto the 3D model. A person who has similar age, racial qualities, and build as the modelled skull is used in a 3D rendering process called 'color mapping'.

This process involves photographing the face of the person with similar qualities and using software to merge the three views into one strip that is put onto the computer to complete the reconstruction. Just like facial reconstruction, the method does have its limitations.

Nose, mouth and ear shape are largely down to estimation, however, lighting conditions and the ability to view the face from any angle makes computer facial reconstruction very lifelike and helpful during investigations.

JOHN GEORGE HAIGH

No chapter on the identification of skeletal remains would be complete without reference to British serial killer John George Haigh. Known as the *Acid Bath Murderer*, John was known to murder his victims and then immerse them in acid rendering their bones to pure sludge before flushing them down the drains. His *modus operandi* was based on the mistaken belief that unless police could find a body then he could not be convicted of murder.

John George Haigh was born in Stamford, Lincolnshire, in 1909 and grew up in the village of Outwood, West Yorkshire. His parents were members of a conservative Protestant sect who advocated austere lifestyles. He had a lonely childhood and after school had various jobs in a garage, insurance and advertising. In 1934, Haigh married the 23 year-old Beatrice Hammer. The marriage soon fell apart. The same year Haigh was jailed for fraud. He then moved to London in 1936, and became chauffeur to William McSwan. Following that he became a bogus solicitor and received a four-year jail sentence for fraud.

While in prison he dreamed up what he considered the perfect murder of being able to destroy the body by dissolving it with sulphuric acid. When freed he bumped into his former employer, McSwan, in Kensington. McSwan introduced Haigh to his parents, William and Amy. On 6 September 1944, McSwan disappeared. Haigh later admitted hitting him over the head after luring him into a basement at 79 Gloucester Road, London SW7. He then put McSwan's body into a 40-gallon drum and allowed it dissolve in sulphuric acid. He poured the resultant sludge down a manhole. When McSwans parents became too curious about his disappearance he lured them to his workshop and disposed of them as well. Haigh fraudulently converted all of the McSwan's assets to his own use.

In 1947 he found another couple to kill and rob: Dr. Archibald Henderson and his wife Rose. They were killed in the same manner at his premises 2 Leopold Road, Crawley, West Sussex. He also converted all their property to his own use.

Haigh's next and last victim was Olive Durand-Deacon, 69, a wealthy widow. On 18 February 1949, he lured her to his workshop in Crawley, shot her in the back of the head, and put her into the acid bath. When she was reported missing Haigh was arrested and immediately confessed that he had not only killed Durand-Deacon, the McSwans and Hendersons, but also three other people.

It was the murder of Olive Durand-Deacon at 2 Leopold Road Crawley which was his undoing. As there was no main drains on the premises John decided to simply spread the Mrs. Durand-Deacon's sludge around the grounds of the yard.

Despite the confession the police still had to prove that even though they didn't have any bodies that Haigh had committed the murders. And so, one of the first ever forensic investigations was undertaken. Following Haigh's initial confession, the West Sussex chief constable requested help from Scotland Yard in the form of a chief inspector and a pathologist. Chief-Inspector Mahon assumed charge of the case. Mahon accompanied Dr. Keith Simpson and Inspector Symes to the storehouse in Crawley where Haigh had carried out his "experiments."

Their objective was to ascertain if any physical evidence could be extracted from the crime scene which would help the prosecution in their case. Questions concerning Haigh's sanity were now beginning to surface and Scotland Yard knew that further corroborating evidence from a forensic examination of the site would be crucial.

On examining the yard outside the storehouse Police found the acid sludge that Haigh had described. They noticed a lot of zigzag marks from where someone had rolled and dragged something heavy over toward that area.

Their search was made more difficult as the ground was covered in debris and the sludge was mixed up with dirt and trash. Its depth was some three to four inches covering an area of four to six feet. However, almost on entering the yard Dr. Simpson's practiced eye detected something unusual, about the size of a cherry, which to anyone else might look like one of the stones lying around. However, it proved to be a significant find.

It was not a cherry; it was, in fact, a human gall bladder stone. Luckily, it had not been dissolved by the acid. He also discovered some good specimens of human bone, including what appeared to be the remnants of someone's left foot.

Al in all, the forensic team gathered four hundred and seventy five pounds of grease and earth and had it carted back to the police laboratory for closer inspection. They also brought in a forty gallon green drum that had the same greasy substance inside. At the bottom of this drum, a hairpin was stuck in the grease.

Further evidence was discovered inside the storehouse. A fine spatter of bloodstains was noted on the wall and carefully photographed. The wall was then scraped for analysis. Inspector Shelley Symes believed that the spray was consistent with someone getting shot while bent over the bench, possibly looking at some papers.

This was exactly how Haigh had described the shooting of Mrs. Durand-Deacon. Although subsequent tests proved the blood was human a blood group could not be specified. Scientists wearing rubber gloves, with their arms covered in Vaseline to protect themselves from the acid, carefully sifted through the sludge over a period of three days.

The painstaking search paid off. All in all they found:

Twenty eight pounds of human body fat;
Three faceted gallstones;
Portion of a human left foot;
Eighteen fragments of human bone;
Intact upper and lower dentures;
The handle of a red plastic bag; and
A lipstick container.

The next step was to match the items discovered with the victims he had murdered.

The red plastic strap was identified as belonging to the handbag carried by Mrs. Durand-Deacon when she left to keep her appointment with Haigh on the 18 February. Fortunately, sulfuric acid did not work on plastic as it did on human tissue. It would take at least three weeks for the acid to finally eliminate it. Thus, if Haigh had been arrested later or had chosen to wait with his confession, the forensic team would have had much less success in finding identifiable evidence. Later, the rest of the bag was found in the yard and matched to the strap.

The bone fragments were identified as a left ankle pivot

bone, center of the right foot, right heel, right angle pivot bone, femur, pelvic bone, spinal column, and others too eroded for precise identification. They had been dissolved in sulfuric acid, just as Haigh had described.

In his laboratory at Guy's Hospital, London, Simpson identified most of the bone fragments as human and in some joints he detected the presence of osteoarthritis. He soon determined that Mrs. Durand-Deacon had suffered from this bone ailment.

Meanwhile, the police had made a plaster cast of the left foot and checked it against a shoe belonging to Mrs. Durand-Deacon; it was a perfect fit.

Mrs. Durand-Deacon's gum shrinkage problems had sent her to her dentist, Mrs. Helen Mayo, on many occasions. Mrs. Mayo kept a cast of her patient's upper and lower jaw. She examined the dentures and confirmed that she had fitted her patient with them two years earlier.

Obviously, Haigh was unaware that the dentures were acrylic and therefore unusually resistant to the corrosive action of acids.

Bloodstains were also found on a Persian coat, which was traced back to Mrs. Durand-Deacon from repairs made to it. The blood on the coat and blood found on the cuff of one of Haigh's shirtsleeves were a perfect match.

The scientific investigation was methodical. Another member of the forensic team, Dr. Turfitt began experimenting with sulfuric acid to test Haigh's theories. He used an amputated human foot, a sheep's leg, and other organic materials. As a result of these experiments, he discovered that the acid worked at varying speeds, depending on how much water was present. Fat proved highly resistant. It was now apparent that it had been Mrs. Durand-Deacon's weight that had preserved those items found in the sludge.

This complete forensic identification gave the lie to Haigh's perfect crime. But despite the forensic evidence it was his own sense of invincibility and arrogance that was to be his greatest undoing and that would damage his case. Haigh was still of the opinion that nothing could be found from his human slaughterhouse and cockily recounted, in great detail, his escapades of death.

As far as he was concerned, it was a case of *corpus delicti*. No bodies, no crime, no punishment. As far as the police were concerned it was a charge of murder, a trial and conviction and an appointment with executioner, Albert Pierrepoint.

Following his trial he was duly convicted and executed. The moral of the story is that even if you dispose of a body in sulphuric acid causing it to turn to sludge there will always be certain matters which will not dissolve. Had he flushed the sludge down a main drain it would have been next to impossible for the police to have conducted such a successful forensic investigation.

11 IDENTIFYING DECAYING BODIES

"We get a lot of calls where the person is murdered at home, but is not found for a period of time. And so the animals have already started to take the body apart because they haven't been fed in that period. So your evidence is being chewed up by the family pet. I tell you - Dogs are more loyal than cats. Cats will wait only a certain period of time and they'll start chewing on you. Dogs will wait a day or two before they just can't take the starving anymore. So, keep that in mind when choosing a pet."
Connie Fletcher, *Every Contact Leaves a Trace*

Sometimes a body is in the process of decomposing when it is found. This is where entomology comes in. Basically, entomology is the study of insects. However, we are concerned here with forensic entomology which is the study of insects and other arthropods in a legal context.

The applications for forensic entomology are wide-ranging, but it is most usually used to determine the minimum time since death where that death has occurred in suspicious circumstances. This is sometimes referred to as the PMI or post-mortem interval. Entomologist try to determine this time by identifying the age of the insects present on a human corpse. If a forensic pathologist is unable to determine the estimated time of death due to insect infestation then the chances are that a forensic entomologist might still be able to provide a relatively precise estimate.

This is based on the fundamental assumption that the body has not been dead for longer than it took the insects to arrive at the corpse and develop. Accordingly, the entomologist will examine the age of the largest and therefore the oldest insects on the body in order to ascertain the minimum PMI.

If a body has been *in situ* for a while then the likelihood is that it has been colonized by several different types of insects. Blowflies or bluebottles are usually the first to colonize a body after death and arrive within a matter of hours. Their presence on the corpse is in accordance with their natural role in the environment as primary decomposers. Although they may look chaotic and gruesome, larval infestations are a vital component of the natural re-cycling of organic matter. They can also provide vital clues to the timing and cause of death on a human body. Blowflies will not be the only species to attack the body. One should also expect to find other species of fly, beetle, wasp and moth arriving after the blowflies.

Where a body has been uninjured you should expect the blowflies to lay eggs in the natural orifices such as the ears, mouth, eyes and nose as well as any other places which are dark and moist. This would include underneath the body or in the folds of their clothes. Where maggots are discovered at sites other than these then it may be the site of an injury which would suggest that some traumatic wounding was inflicted on the body prior to death.

Various factors are taken into consideration in determining the time of death. For example, generally egg laying takes place in daylight, so if death occurs at night, laying will be delayed. If the body is buried or if the body is discovered inside then the flies will take longer to discover it. Weather conditions also must be factored in. If the conditions are moderately dry, then the eggs hatch into first instar larvae about eight hours after laying.

They grow rapidly with the second instar occurring about twenty four hours later and the third instar about twenty hours after that. After about five days the larvae stops feeding and rest. After a few more days the larva transforms into a pupa and emerges as an adult fly three weeks after the eggs were laid.

Depending on what species is involved they either pupate on the body or move away to find a suitable site. Outside, they may move many meters before burrowing into the soil or under objects such as rocks and logs. Indoors, they usually settle under carpets and furniture. The larva then contracts and the cuticle hardens and darkens to form the barrel-shaped puparium within which, the pupa transforms into an adult fly.

When the fly is born it leaves behind the empty puparial case as long-lasting evidence of the insect's development. Blowflies have four life stages: egg, larva or maggot, pupa and adult. The larval stage is divided into three instars. In between each instar the larva sheds its cuticle (skin) to allow for growth in the next instar. The pupa is a transition stage between larva and adult. It is found inside a barrel shaped puparium, which is actually the hardened and darkened skin of the final instar larva.

Temperature and ambient conditions are the crucial factors which determine how quickly insects develop. Very generally speaking, as this varies between species, the higher the temperature, the faster the insects will develop; the lower the temperature, the slower they will develop. If the ambient temperatures during the period of development are known, then, in theory, it should be possible to determine the minimum PMI.

WHAT DOES A FORENSIC ENTOMOLOGIST DO?

Forensic entomologists have to determine facts about the location of the body and its accessibility to flies at the scene of the crime. They will collect specimens of the complete range of maggots present on and near the body. If they are not available at the crime scene this function may be performed by the forensic pathologist or even a trained scene of crime officer. They will specifically note the location of the maggots *vis-à-vis* the body, the time of collection and the ambient temperature.

The specimens are then brought to the lab where they are killed by immersing them in water heated to slightly below boiling point. To prevent discoloration and shrinkage they are then transferred to a solution of 80% ethanol.

Taxonomic identification of the insects found on corpses is crucial in endeavoring to reconstruct events surrounding a suspicious death. Systems of classification of biological organisms are used to facilitate their identification.

The forensic entomologist then determines the age of the specimens to provide evidence of when the female flies first found the body and laid their eggs. Once he has determined the age he can then deduce a minimum estimate of the post mortem interval. This can be taken as the latest time by which death must have occurred.

Because the blowfly is cold blooded they develop more slowly at lower temperatures than they do at higher temperatures. The forensic entomologist will attempt to estimate the hourly temperature at the discovery site for the period over which the maggots were developing. He will arrive at the time of egg laying by taking account of varying daily temperatures.

Generally, size is a function of age, in that, up to the post-feeding stage, the larger the maggot the older it is. But it is not as simple as that as size can also be affected by the amount of food available as well as the number of maggots competing for that food. If food resources decrease as the maggot population increases then this could result in a decrease in the average size of the maggots present. This is why it is so important to collect a full range of maggot sizes present on the corpse.

Another factor which might affect the rate of development of feeding larvae may be if any toxic substances are in or on the dead body. If, for example, the victim has recently taken heroin or cocaine then their presence can significantly increase the development rate of larvae. Conversely, insects may take much longer to colonize and decompose a body if that body is wearing clothes which are permeated with materials such as paint, oil or combustibles.

Consideration will also be given to the general geographical location of the discovery site of the body. Insects have known habitat preferences and known geographical distributions. Knowing these can assist in arriving at conclusions about the type of place, a river bank, woodland, open pasture or indoors, in which the body has been previously lying, as well as the part of the country from where it originated.

The burial of a body presents its own difficulties. It will effectively isolate it from many of the insects usually associated with decomposition. This, in turn, will have significant effects on the estimation of an accurate PMI. Even if a body has only be buried in a shallow grave with a covering of as little as 2.5 cm of soil then this can significantly delay decomposition. The reason for this because blowflies very rarely lay their eggs on the surface of the soil. They prefer instead to lay them on the corpse itself.

The insect colonization of a buried corpse may also be affected by soil type, its permeability to odors of decay, and the ease with which insects can move through it. Generally speaking it is much more difficult to determine the PMI in cases where bodies have been buried but the evidence acquired may still give a good indication of events that occurred prior to the burial, like how long it was exposed above ground after death. In this regard, entomologists will be searching for what are called coffin flies. Their presence is a reliable indicator of when a body has been previously buried then exhumed and placed on the surface.

Circumstances where there is little or no insect infestation can also assist murder investigations. For example, the lack of blowfly larvae on a week old corpse found in the open in the height of summer would indicate that the murder had taken place elsewhere and that the body had only recently been dumped in that location. An entomologist can also help in relation to post mortem marks on a body. Sometimes these can be caused by the bites and secretions of insects such as ants, beetles or earwigs.

Furthermore, an assailant may have collected small insects and other organisms on his clothes or shoes or they may be found in his vehicle thus indicating that he may have been in the general area of the crime. Sometimes bodies are weighed down and dumped in the sea or in lakes. Fans of the serial killer series *Dexter* will be aware that he always disposed of his bodies by dumping them at sea. Is this a good way to conceal a body?

A body dumped at sea or in a lake will also suffer from colonization by aquatic organisms and they too can be used to estimate how long a body has been submerged in water. Such investigation techniques are much more advanced in American than they are in Europe.

FORENSIC BOTANY & THE LOCARD PRINCIPLE

Forensic botany is another field which has developed recently. Based on the Locard exchange principle first articulated in 1910 by French forensic scientist Edmond Locard it states that every contact leaves a trace.

It has been eloquently described in the following terms by Paul L. Kirk in his book *Crime investigation: physical evidence and the police laboratory* (1953):

"Wherever he steps, whatever he touches, whatever he leaves, even unconsciously, will serve as a silent witness against him. Not only his fingerprints or his footprints, but his hair, the fibers from his clothes, the glass he breaks, the tool mark he leaves, the paint he scratches, the blood or semen he deposits or collects. All of these and more, bear mute witness against him. This is evidence that does not forget. It is not confused by the excitement of the moment. It is not absent because human witnesses are. It is factual evidence. Physical evidence cannot be wrong, it cannot perjure itself, it cannot be wholly absent. Only human failure to find it, study and understand it, can diminish its value."

In forensic botany it is often the case that trace botanical evidence can link an object or suspect to the scene of a crime, as well as rule out a suspect or support an alibi. In some cases, a plant's anatomy and its ecological requirements are species-specific.

Correct interpretation of botanical evidence can provide crucial information about a crime scene and or clues to the whereabouts of a suspect or victim. Sometimes vegetation is associated with the remains or the crime scene. Forensic botanists can determine if a body has been removed from its original resting place. They can also help determine the type of area it came from. Plants can be identified through microscopic characteristics such as seeds and spores. As in the case of insects, many plants grow exclusively in specific areas and within localized ecosystems.

Some experts argue that ultimately the value of botanical evidence in a forensic investigation depends on what happened or was missed at the crime scene. But they will be unable to use their plant analysis to resolve a critical issue if a CS investigator or technician failed to start the process.

12 POISONS

"I just wanted them to die," said Poison. "They didn't have to make such a drama about it."
Chris Wooding, *Poison*

Forensic toxicology can be described as that branch of forensic science which seeks to identify and quantify the presence of toxins in the human body. A forensic toxicologist is likely to take samples of blood, urine, various other biological fluids, hair, nails and other tissues for examination. Such examinations are carried out in forensic laboratories under the jurisdiction of government agencies, or in private laboratories certified by government agencies for such practices.

The purpose of forensic toxicology is to obtain analytical data on toxins with a view to applying that data to the understanding of an episode of intoxication. In their paper *Toxicology, Mechanisms and Analytical Methods,* Vol. 1. Academic Press, New York, 1961 Stewart and Stolman (1961) put it this way "the forensic toxicologist has a 'dual objective of identifying qualitatively and determining quantitatively' poisonous substances in species of human origin, and that, furthermore, he must 'interpret his results in such a way that the maximal amount of information may be derived from them.'" This, in essence, is the purpose of forensic toxicology, to obtain analytical data on poisons and to apply the information obtained to the understanding of an episode of intoxication.

The role of the forensic toxicologist is to examine samples of blood and urine and determine whether or not an individual has been using, or is under the influence of an illegal narcotic substance as in, for example, the police or armed forces. But they may also be instructed to examine blood, urine and tissue samples taken from a corpse in order to determine if they have died as a result of drugs or other illicit chemicals. Such an examination will assist investigators in determining if death occurred as a result of accidental death, suicide or homicide. Accidental death occurs most usually in cases where infants have ingested material which they thought represented food like, for example poison berries, medicines that resemble candy, and drinks like petrol and bleach stored in soft drink bottles.

There are approximately 30,000 cases of attempted suicide in Britain every year with tranquilizers, carbon monoxide, and barbiturates accounting for approximately 90% of all suicides. Barbiturates are drugs that act as central nervous system depressants. They can produce a wide range of effects from mild sedation to total anesthesia

There has been a decrease in the amount of people poisoned in homicide cases over the last number of decades. This is due to both increased regulation in the availability of a wide range of poisons and advances in developing laboratory detection techniques. However, for some people in certain situations, there are opportunities to use toxins as a murder weapon with an increased degree of impunity. Medical practitioners are a case in point with Dr. Harold Shipman being responsible for the murder of several hundred deaths of his patients through poisoning.

The first step in the process of a toxicological investigation is the extraction of a sample. But before any analysis of that sample can take place the sample has first to be treated so as to extract and purify the poison in it. If toxins are, in fact, present the amount will be very small as most poisons are fatal in low doses. Depending on their nature, poisons can be extracted using organic solvents, such as ether or chloroform, or by the use of solid silica absorbents.

Usually sample are taken from the following fluids and tissues:

Urine: This is the most common type of sample taken from living persons as it produces fast and simple results for live subjects. It is most commonly used for drug testing law enforcement (dui, drink driving) cases, employees and athletes. Urine can reveal traces of some substances for several weeks after their introduction into the body, for example, marijuana. This drug will take two weeks to clear your system. The sample is taken from the bladder in the case of a dead person or provided by a live person. Urine is less likely to be infected with viruses such as HIV or Hepatitis B than blood samples. Many drugs have a higher concentration and can remain for much longer in urine than blood which is why some people opt for a blood sample as opposed to a urine sample in road traffic cases. It should be noted that urine is used for qualitative analysis as it cannot give any indication of impairment due to the fact that drug presence in urine only indicates prior exposure.

Blood: A quantity of 10 cubic centimeters of blood (0.35 imperial fluid oz; 0.34 US fluid oz) is required to screen and confirm the presence of most toxic substances. Blood sample differ from urine samples in that unlike urine samples, the blood sample screen will actually provide the list of toxic substances such as morphine, heroin and anti-depressants present in the body at the time of collection.

Saliva: The concentration of the toxic substances present in saliva is in parallel to that of the blood. The use of oral fluids is becoming increasingly more popular in the fields of clinical settings and drink driving cases.

Lungs: Solvents and other hazardous chemicals collect in the lungs.

Hair: The hair is an important sample in the field of forensic toxicology. Hair is capable of recording medium to long-term or high dosage substance abuse. Chemicals in the bloodstream may be transferred to the growing hair and stored in the follicle. This can provide a rough timeline of drug intake events. As head hair normally grows at rate of approximately 1 to 1.5 cm per month, cross sections from different sections of the follicle can give estimates as to when a substance was introduced into the body. But it is important to know that testing for drugs in hair is not standard throughout the population. When tested more drugs will be found in people with darker and coarser hair than those with lighter and fairer hair.

As well as the above, other body fluids and body organs are collected during an autopsy which can provide vital information. Stomach contents of the deceased person are a useful sample in determining the presence of undigested pills or liquids that were introduced into the body just before death. Other samples can be taken from the brain, liver, spleen and the vitreous humor behind the eye.

If the body is decomposed the forensic toxicologist will consider taking samples from the insects which have colonized the body.

As well as taking samples, a forensic toxicologist must consider the context of the investigation, not just any physical symptoms recorded, but also any evidence collected at a crime scene, such as pill bottles, powders, trace residue, and any available chemicals. He should also consider other issues before drawing his conclusions. For example, the concentration of a poison or a metabolite will vary depending from where in the circulatory system the blood sample was taken. Samples taken from urine can vary widely from person to person and even in the same person depending upon the state of that person's hydration. Furthermore, urine is affected by how much water a person may have drunk in that the more water they have drunk the more diluted the drug contained in it will be. Usually a toxicologist will not be called upon to express an opinion of whether the toxin levels in the body were enough to cause death although those with the appropriate training and qualification in physiology may be called to do so. But, in the main, opinions on cause of death are normally the province of a forensic pathologist.

The detection of drugs in the system is a dual system of first screening and later confirmation and quantification. Both the screening and the confirmation are carried out using different analytical methods. Every analytical method in forensic toxicology must be carefully tested with a pre-forming validation of the method to ensure the correct and indisputable results each time. Any testing laboratory involved in forensic pathology is obliged to adhere to some strict policies to ensure the best possible results and safety of every individual.

There are three basic testing techniques used:

Immunoassay testing;
TLC or thin layer chromatography; and
Gas chromatography and mass spectrometry.

Immunoassay tests can be described as simple chemical tests which are used to detect or quantify a specific substance, the analyte, in a blood or body fluid sample, using an immunological reaction. The tests are highly sensitive and specific and are used to detect substances such as barbiturates, cocaine and other drugs. Their high specificity results from the use of antibodies and purified antigens as reagents.

In an immunoassay kit the artificial antibodies react with

the chemicals in a body fluid such as urine and brings about a change in color which indicates the presence of toxins. The toxicologist will then perform a more thorough laboratory test to identify the toxins.

TLC is a simple, fast, and inexpensive procedure that gives the toxicologist a quick answer as to how many components are in a mixture and to support the identity of a compound in a mixture. A TLC plate is a sheet of either glass, metal, or plastic which is coated with a thin layer of a solid adsorbent, in most cases, silica or alumina. A small amount of the mixture to be analyzed is spotted near the bottom of this plate. The plate is then lowered into a shallow pool of a solvent in a developing chamber so that only the very bottom of the plate is in the liquid. This liquid, or the eluent, is the mobile phase.

Gradually it will ascend up the TLC plate by capillary action. As the liquid passes the spot that was applied, an equilibrium is established for each component of the mixture, between the molecules of that component, which are adsorbed on the solid, and the molecules which are in solution. In principle, the components will differ in solubility and in the strength of their adsorption to the adsorbent and some components will be carried farther up the plate than others.

When the liquid reaches the top of the plate, the plate is removed from the developing chamber, dried, and the separated components of the mixture are examined. If the compounds are colored then examination or visualization as it is called is simple enough. However, usually the compounds are not colored. It then becomes necessary to use a UV lamp to visualize the plates.

The third testing tool is gas chromatography and mass spectrometry. This is the single most important method used to identify and quantify volatile and semi-volatile organic compounds in complex mixtures. The method is used for the quantitation of drugs and their metabolites in blood and urine. The sample is vaporized and mixed with a neutral carrier gas such as nitrogen. It is then passed through a filter like a Perspex tube filled with granules.

The toxicologist then measures the speed at which the constituent parts of the vaporized gas reach the sensor at the end of the tube. This speed will reveal the identity of the individual elements which are shown as peaks of various intensity on a digital graphic display. The gas chromatograph is often supported by a mass spectrometer. The purpose of the mass spectrometer is to isolate ions (charged particles) which are then measured to create a spectrum which identifies their chemical make-up.

13 FRAUD: DISPUTED DOCUMENTS

"They look upon fraud as a greater crime than theft, and therefore seldom fail to punish it with death; for they allege, that care and vigilance, with a very common understanding, may preserve a man's goods from thieves, but honesty has no defence against superior cunning; and, since it is necessary that there should be a perpetual intercourse of buying and selling, and dealing upon credit, where fraud is permitted and connived at, or has no law to punish it, the honest dealer is always undone, and the knave gets the advantage."
Jonathan Swift, *Gulliver's Travels*

A disputed document is defined as any written or printed communication the source or authenticity of which is in doubt. The term "disputed documents" refers to much more than communications written on paper with pen or pencil and includes communications written in mediums such as blood, paint or lipstick on surfaces such as mirrors, tables, even the side of a house. Disputed documents include forged documents such as passports, driving licenses and money.

This ever growing branch of forensic science assists in the investigation of many types of fraud-related criminal and civil investigations including but not limited to activities such as:

The examination, comparison, and identification of handwriting, signatures, or initials on a wide variety of disputed documents;
The examination, comparison, and identification of typewriters, check writers, printers, and other office machines;
The examination and comparison of inks, pens, markers, and other writing media;
The examination of documents to decipher and interpret relevant facts about alterations, erasures, obliterations or

substitutions on various papers;

The examination, decipherment and comparison of indented writings;

The examination, comparison, and identification of faxed, scanned and photocopied documents;

Consultations, advice, and technical support for forgery and fraud investigations;

The physical matching and reconstruction of torn, charred, water-damaged or mutilated documents; and,

The investigation of checks and related negotiable instruments to determine the authenticity of signatures or determination of alterations and additions. These would represent the main areas involved.

Accordingly, a disputed documents expert should have training, knowledge and expertise in everything to do with handwriting, printing, typewriting, papers, inks and different methods used to alter and obliterate writing.

All questioned document evidence can be categorized into three main areas:

Handwriting;
Typewritten documents; and,
Printed documents.

Handwriting analysis is the oldest and most challenging type of disputed document examination. Even despite the increasing use of computers in modern day business, handwriting remains a classic example of the principles and issues arising from pattern evidence. Although there may be many similarities no two people share exactly the same type of handwriting. Our handwriting is a very personal attribute whose uniqueness forms the basis of handwriting identification. But, it is not simply your handwriting as you write now which may have to be examined but also the fluctuations in your style over time a period of time through age or even illness. Other relevant factors that must be taken into consideration include tiredness, the use of alcohol or medication and even your emotional state. Despite all of these factors, the basic style should be evident to a trained and experienced handwriting expert.

In forensic criminal cases and certain probate cases involving the authenticity of wills and testamentary dispositions, it will be the task of the examiner to determine whether a particular document was written by the testator. This involves the comparison of documents in dispute with samples of documents not in dispute. The expert will begin by comparing gross differences, such as the way certain characters are written between the documents under examination. Although these differences may be plentiful they will not, on their own, be sufficient to establish authorship.

The expert document examiner will have to prepare and present a type of visual description of the different sets of handwriting being compared. He will do this by using the relative positions of the highest and lowest points of the letters to produce a picture of what might be termed the amplitude of the writing.

Examination is based on several accepted principles. As stated above, although there may be many similarities no two people have the same handwriting. There is a natural variation in a person's handwriting. No single writing characteristic is so unique by itself that it will individualize handwriting.

Also, no person writes the same letter or number exactly the same way twice. Accordingly, in order to allow the expert observe the range of variations in the handwriting he will need to examine several samples. Finally, no set number of characteristics exist that must be present for an examiner to identify the author of a disputed document

When there is no undisputed sample for comparison a difficulty will present itself but this may be overcome by asking the suspect to write a piece of text which the expert will dictate. Of course an unscrupulous suspect could use this as an opportunity to deliberately alter his handwriting to deceive the investigation. Nevertheless, certain basic aspects of handwriting style are automatic and cannot be changed that simply.

So what represents a match? This is not as scientific as perhaps it should be but experts tend to use and accept a five point scale when deciding if someone was the author of a document or not. This highly subjective means of arriving at a conclusion is rated on a scale from common authorship to no evidence. Common authorship arises when there is 100% positivity that the documents have been written by the same person. The next scale is one of high probability where there is very strong positive evidence and where it is very unlikely to have been written by someone else. The third point on the scale is where it probably could well have been written by the same person. Finally, there is inconclusive evidence and no evidence.

ALTERATIONS

Many forgeries consist of alterations to documents and there are several tests which can easily prove these alterations. Such alterations may involve the removal of a word or words by erasure or by scraping of the paper. If this has been carried out in a "professional" manner by an expert forger then the alteration will not be easily detected by the naked eye.

But a document expert will dust the document with

lycopodium powder whilst holding it at an angle. When the excess powder is shaken off, some of the powder adheres to the small particles of rubber that have remained on the paper after the erasure has been affected. But this method does not work where plastic erasers have been used.

The use of chemical oxidizing agents or solvents to obliterate words on documents so that a different word can be detected is often revealed by a discoloration of the paper in the treated area. Although it cannot be seen by the naked eye, it will be seen in any microscopic examination of the document.

INK AND INK COLORS

Instrumental techniques for analysis and information gathering are used where a more detailed analysis of the ink dyes, paper and chemical treatments of disputed documents are required. There are various technical ways in which ink and ink colors can be analyzed. A simple thin layer chromatography (TLC) run can easily separate the components of inks and dyes, allowing individual components to be isolated, extracted and subjected to more detailed analysis. If a manufacturer can be matched to the questioned ink or dye, an expert may then be able to identify the type of pen or printer used to produce the document in question. This information is helpful in eliminating suspects.

Another tool that document experts use is called an EDA or electrostatic detection apparatus. This can help detect the indentations on a piece of paper that was below the disputed document when it was written upon. Here, the indented sheet is subjected to an electrostatic field, and charged electrons from the static field are attracted to the damaged or impressed fibers in the paper where the indentations were made. Black toner which is attracted to the damaged areas is applied to the paper and fixed in place allowing the writing to become pronounced. The impressed page is then photographed. The principle underlying EDA is similar to that used by photocopiers or laser printers.

Finally, a video spectral comparator may be used. This is an advanced digital imaging device which uses a variety of oblique, direct and transmitted illumination of various light sources. These could be white light, ultra violet light or infra-red light. A digital camera and computer interface can then analyze the spectral output of the document or inks in question.

MODERN INKS AND DYES

Essentially, there are four different types of modern ink:

Ball point ink;
Iron ink;
Carbon black ink; and
Dyestuck ink.

Modern ball points contain ink based on polyethylene glycol with soluble synthetic dyes or insoluble pigments; The ink is approximately 45% dye and the rest solvents and additives. Iron inks contain iron salts, dye material, Gallic and tannic acid. Carbon black ink or Indian ink as it is commonly called is a suspension of carbon in gum-Arabic.

Finally, dyestuff inks are colored inks, generally labelled non-permanent. They contain aniline dyes, gum-Arabic, glycol, polyethylene and sulphuric or hydrochloric acid.

Examination of inks can provide a rich source of evidence of forgery. Some become transparent under infrared light while others do not. Even where inks absorb infrared light, different inks have different abilities to do so. If you use infrared light and record the light reflected from it on to a special film it may show that different inks have been used.

TYPEWRITERS

Although not so prevalent in today's computer age typewriter comparison may also be used. The most valuable forensic evidence that can be deduced from a typewritten document is which individual machine it was typed upon. Although when they are first manufactured typewriters will have some slight imperfections like the casting of the characters, the greater proportion of identifying characteristics acquired by a machine will occur during its working life.

Letters will become worn or chipped; alignments can be disturbed by frequent and heavy use causing slanting backwards or forwards or perhaps an uneven printed page; the shift key could become damaged and any or all of these will help identify an individual typewriter. Even electric typewriters will have similar distinctive patterns of wear.

One of the prosecution's strongest pieces of evidence against the British serial killer Dr. Harold Shipman related to documents he had typed on his typewriter.

PRE-PRINTED FORMS

Similar comparisons can be carried out on mechanically printed forms and the same comparative principles apply.

The disputed document that contains printing also bears traces of the flourishes and uniqueness of the printer from whence it came.

INKJET AND LASER PRINTERS

While inkjet and laser printers, photocopiers and thermal imaging machines do not use an impression interface as in typewriting they do rely on ionic forces, micro jets or piezoelectric heating. Even though there is a lack of impression evidence on modern printouts, there is still a large amount of individual data that is present on most printed forms and can be identified by microscope.

Any dirt, debris, nick or gouge in printers that have a metal drum for imaging can result in a unique and reproducible trace on every printout. This can be noticed in laser printers, photocopiers and thermal imagers as black spots, blots or lines on the printed surface. For ink jet printers, defects in the print head can result in smears, lines or voids in a printed image.

PAPER

Paper is easier to detect than you might think. Most paper is made from wood pulp but some use linen and cotton and various vegetable fibers. But in the case of security papers, such as currency, special additives are used to make forgeries easier to detect. Fibers used in the manufacture of paper are frequently filled with fine mineral chalk to give the paper greater opacity, less absorbency and more bulk. The surface of the paper may be treated by heat rolling, sizing, starching, or with synthetic resins. In this way the security paper will become unique. This is why expert forgers tend to use existing currency paper and bleach the paper before imprinting their particular forgery.

A microscopic examination of any paper will disclose information about the type of tree from which the wood pulp was obtained, and since more than one type of wood pulp is used in the manufacture of paper, areas of similarity between different papers decreases. Furthermore, in certain manufacturing watermark patterns are molded into the continuous roll, which can identify not only the paper mill of origin but even the type and brand of paper. Because it is put into the paper during manufacture, it is impossible for the forger to make an exact reproduction of the watermark.

14 CYBER CRIME

Cyber crime is a vast area and to deal with it comprehensively would take at least one hundred pages but let's deal with the general principles and with one particular scenario. Envisage the scene where you have a vicious neighbor who convinces the local law enforcement agency that you have been involved in cyber crimes. This could be anything from child pornography to electronic embezzlement to corporate fraud to hacking into state agency computers. You wake up one morning and a detective tells you he has reason to believe you have committed a crime involving a computer or computer related device and he is here to interview you and to search and seize. What can he take? What will he take? What will he do? What can he find?

To begin with, computer-based electronic evidence is subject to the same rules, regulations and laws that apply to documentary evidence. The doctrine of documentary evidence may be explained as: the placing of the onus on the prosecution to show to the court that the evidence produced is no more and no less now than when it was first taken into the possession of police. In Britain, ACPO have produced four principles similar to those found in other jurisdictions, to guide the forensic computer examiner. There are four basic principles:

1. No action taken by law enforcement agencies or their agents should change data held on a computer or storage media which may subsequently be relied upon in court.

2. In circumstances where a person finds it necessary to access original data held on a computer or on storage media, that person must be competent to do so and be able to give evidence explaining the relevance and the implications of their actions.

3. An audit trail or other record of all processes applied to computer-based electronic evidence should be created and preserved. An independent third party should be able to examine those processes and achieve the same result.

4. The person in charge of the investigation (the case officer) has overall responsibility for ensuring that the law and these principles are adhered to.

SEARCH WARRANTS

You will be presented with a Search Warrant. Read it. Carefully. If there are any material mistakes you can point them out and refuse entry. They will usually leave and return with a new one, but it will take a couple of hours. The warrant application should clearly indicate what electronic evidence is involved and which persons are required to expedite the recovery and seizure of that material. Where there is concern that special procedure material is to be part of the electronic evidence, that should also be disclosed. The three most important matters to check on a search warrant are:

1. The name of the person the subject of the Search Warrant;
2. The dates on the Search Warrants indicating when the search may take place;
3. The address to which the Search Warrant relates. It must be specific. "Mr. John Doe, Chelsea, London" will not suffice. "Mr. John Doe, Sloane House Apartments, Sloane Avenue, Chelsea, London" will not suffice. It has to be specific: "Apartment 3A, Sloane House Apartments" would work.
4. The material to be seized. Remember, a computer or associated media should not be seized just because it is there. The person in charge of the search must make a conscious decision to remove property and there must be

a justifiable reason for so doing. But this is an easy obstacle for law enforcers to overcome. If the Search Warrant is later proved to be invalid the likelihood is that any evidence procured on foot of it will not be admissible in court.

The rules appertaining to search warrants in America and in Britain are similar but not identical.

SEARCH WARRANTS IN BRITAIN

In Britain search warrants are issued by a local Magistrate and require a Constable to provide evidence to support the warrant application. In the vast majority of cases where the police already hold someone in custody, a search can be made without a search warrant under Section 18 of the Police and Criminal Evidence Act (PACE). It simply requires only the authority of a Police Inspector. Under a Section 18(5) a search can be conducted immediately by a Constable without the requirement for an Inspector's authorization allowing him to search the address of a suspect under arrest in their presence before being presented to a police station. Section 32 allows a Constable to immediately search a person and property if a person is arrested on their own property or just after leaving their premises. Furthermore, gas company officials may enter a home to inspect, repair or replace gas meters by obtaining a warrant.

SEARCH WARRANTS IN AMERICA

Different states have different laws but in general and subject to certain exceptions, most police searches in America require a search warrant based on probable cause pursuant to the Fourth Amendment to the United States Constitution.

Any police entry into a suspect's home always requires:
(a) a warrant (for either search or arrest);
(b) absent exigent circumstances;
(c) or the free and voluntary consent of a person with reasonably apparent use of or control over the property.

Under the Fourth Amendment, searches must be reasonable and specific. This means that a search warrant must be specific as to the specified object to be searched for and the place to be searched. Other items, rooms, outbuildings, persons, vehicles, usually require additional search warrants if they are not specified on the warrant.

To obtain a search warrant, an officer must first prove to the judge that probable cause exists. This proof must be based upon direct information, that is, obtained by the officer's personal observation or solid hearsay information. Hearsay information can even be obtained by oral testimony given over a telephone, or through an anonymous or confidential informant, so long as probable cause exists based on the totality of the circumstances.

Both property and persons can be seized under a search warrant. The standard for a search warrant is lower than the quantum of proof required for a later conviction. The rationale is that the evidence that can be collected without a search warrant may not be sufficient to convict, but may be sufficient to suggest that enough evidence to convict could be found using the warrant. Search warrants will not be given as "fishing exercises."

But remember that American Police do not need a search warrant, or even probable cause, to perform a limited search of a suspect's outer clothing for weapons, providing that police have a reasonable suspicion to justify the intrusion.

The issue of federal warrants in America is determined under Title 18 of the United States Code. The law has been restated and extended under Rule 41 of the Federal Rules of Criminal Procedure. Federal search warrants may be prepared on Form AO 93, Search and Seizure Warrant. Each individual state also enacts its own laws governing the issuance of search warrants.

An exception arises in relation to Customs and Immigration officials. Under 19 U.S.C. 1467, 19 C.F.R. 162.6. a customs or immigration officer of the United States is not required to have any warrant, reasonable suspicion, or consent to search persons, vehicles, baggage, or cargo that have border nexus; regardless of their citizenship or origin.

It is important to remember that there are also other exceptions. No warrant is required where consent is given by a person in control of the object or property to be searched.

Other examples would be where the police are in hot pursuit of a suspect and need to prevent his escape or ability to harm others; where they is the imminent destruction of evidence before a warrant can be properly obtained; where an emergency search is necessary, where for example, there is a call for help from inside the building; or where there is evidence in plain view from a legitimate vantage point, and it is immediately obvious that the evidence is contraband.

CYBER CRIME SEARCHES

The investigators will bring all or some of the following items to assist them in their search: a property register; exhibit labels; labels and tape to mark and identify component parts of the system, including leads and sockets; tools such as screw drivers (flathead and crosshead), small pliers, wire cutters for removal of cable ties; a range of packaging and evidential bags fit for the purpose of securing and sealing heavy items such as computers and smaller items such as PDAs and mobile phone handsets; cable ties for securing cables; flat pack assembly boxes; colored marker pens to code and identify removed items; and a camera and/or video to photograph scene in situ and any on-screen displays.

This may also bring a Pro-Forma sheet on which they will complete information such as a sketch map of the scene; details of all persons present where computers are located; details of computers, that is, make, model, serial number; display details and connected peripherals; remarks, comments and information offered by users of computer, actions taken at scene showing exact time.

EVIDENCE RECOVERY

The following forensic procedures will be followed: collection, examination, analysis, and reporting. The collection phase involves the search for, recognition of, collection of and documentation of computer-based electronic evidence.

The examination process helps to make the evidence visible and explain its origin and significance and it should accomplish several things. First, it should document the content and state of the evidence in its totality. Such documentation allows all parties to discover what is contained in the evidence. Included in this process is the search for information that may be hidden or obscured. Once all the information is visible, the process of data reduction can begin, thereby separating the "wheat" from the "chaff." Given the tremendous amount of information that can be stored on electronic media, this part of the examination is critical.

The next phase is the analysis phase. This differs from examination in that it looks at the product of the examination for its significance and probative value to the case.

Examination is a technical review that is the province of the forensic practitioner, while analysis may be conducted by a range of people.

The report or statement outlines the examination process and the pertinent data recovered and completes an examination. The role of the examiner is to secure from any seized material, be it hard disks, floppy disks, tape or any other storage media, a true copy of the data contained therein. This should be obtained without compromising the original data. In order to ensure this, care should be taken in the selection of software or hardware utilized in any procedure that is undertaken.

As the process that is being conducted is a forensic examination, sound and established forensic principles should be adhered to. This means full records should be made of all actions taken. These can be made available to the defense who may subsequently conduct a further examination to validate the actions taken. Such records are also part of the unused material for the case under investigation.

What are they likely to seize? Basically, anything they consider may relate to or be connected with the commission of a crime. This will be desktops, laptops, screen, keyboards, main units, leads, cables, floppy disks, CDs and DVDs. But they may also take PDAs, palmtop computers, next generation games consoles, portable media players and mobile phones incorporating software, removable storage and significant processing power. Furthermore, they are likely to take power supply units; hard disks not fitted inside the computer; dongles; modems; external drives and other external devices; wireless network cards; routers; digital cameras; back-up tapes; jaz/zip cartridges; PCMCIA cards; memory sticks, memory cards and all USB/firewire connected devices.

And it they are really serious expect them also to take manuals of computer and software; *anything* that may contain a password.; encryption keys; security keys; batteries; printers, printouts and printer paper for forensic analysis. Sometimes, if they deem it necessary, and depending on the seriousness of crime they may consider taking pagers; land line telephones; answering machines; fax and dictating machines; telephone e-mailers; internet-capable digital TVs; media PC, HD recorders and even satellite receivers.

What will they do? One thing they will definitely not do is turn on a computer. If this happens then something is seriously wrong. Either they are not the police or they are totally incompetent. What they should do is secure and take control of the area containing the equipment; move people away from any computers and power supplies; photograph or video the scene and all the components including the leads *in situ* or draw a sketch; and allow any printers to finish printing.

They will also search the area for diaries, notebooks or pieces of paper with passwords on which are often attached or close to the computer. They will ask you for the passwords and details about the setup of the system.

As you can see, the amount of evidence they can take away is quite substantial and may even include childrens' computers as these are good places to hide illegal material.

FORENSIC COMPUTER INVESTIGATION

Computer-based electronic evidence is, by its very nature, fragile. It must be dealt with in a professional yet delicate way. It can be altered, damaged, or destroyed by improper handling or improper examination. Accordingly, special precautions should be taken to document, collect, preserve and examine the evidence as failure to do so could result in it being inadmissible or lead to an inaccurate conclusion. Computer investigators require specialized training and tools with which to work. They will need to be *au fait* with the use of advanced search programs, access to sophisticated computer equipment, a working knowledge of evidence recovery methods, and a keen understanding of the types of associated computer evidence that a court will insist on.

A forensic computer investigator knows that there is an increasing amount of data susceptible to forensic examination, by virtue of the fact that the deletion of a file on a computer or other device will not usually result in the underlying data being removed. As the capacity of hard drives and other storage media has grown, the probability that the space previously occupied by a "deleted" file will be overwritten has declined. It is possible for files that were "deleted" years ago to be readily recoverable by use of specialized forensic software. This is also true for hard drives that have been formatted. The process of formatting does not overwrite or remove the underlying data.

How safe are my emails? They aren't. Even if deleted they can be forensically retrieved from physical machines. How safe are my mobile phone messages. Again they aren't. What about other stored data? A number of forensic tools exist that enable investigators to streamline and control their search for evidence in storage devices. For instance, there are a number of specialized search programs that allow investigators to structure and customize searches for important digital evidence. Investigators need to know that encrypted data and various compressed data formats will not allow these types of searches until the data is uncompressed or decrypted.

COMMON INTERNET SCAMS

What are the most common internet scams that criminals use on the internet? That part of the FBI that deals with Cyber Crime is called the Internet Crime Complaints Center or IC3. The European equivalent is called EC3. In its 2013 Annual Report IC3 outlines the current most common internet frauds as follows:

1. **Auto-Auction Fraud** – The IC3 has received a significant number of complaints regarding Internet auction fraud involving the sale of automobiles. Many of these listings are for vehicles located outside the United States. In most cases the criminal attempts to sell vehicles they do not own. Criminals create attractive deals by advertising vehicles at prices below book value. Often criminals claims they must sell the vehicle because they are moving or being relocated for work. Due to the pending move, the criminals often refuse to meet with potential buyers or allow vehicle inspections and ultimately try to rush the sale. In an attempt to make the deal appear legitimate, the criminal often instructs victims to send full or partial payments to third-party agents via wire transfers and to fax their payment receipt to the seller as proof of payment. Once payment is made, the criminal pockets the money and the victim never receives the vehicle.

2. **Romance Scams** – The IC3 continues to receive complaints of romance scams in which scammers target individuals searching for companionship or romance

online. Victims believe they are "dating" a good and honest person without ever physically meeting them. The online contact is often a criminal sitting in a cyber café with a well-rehearsed script used to repeatedly and successfully scam others. Perpetrators of these scams search chat rooms, dating sites, and social networking sites looking for potential targets. Although all demographics are at risk, the group targeted the most appears to be people aged 40 years and older, divorced, widowed, disabled, and often elderly.

Romance scammers use poetry, flowers, and other gifts to draw in their victims. They continuously declare their "undying love" for victims. These criminals also use stories of severe life circumstances, tragedies, family deaths, injuries to themselves, or other hardships to keep their victims concerned and involved in their schemes. Scammers also ask victims to send money to help overcome alleged hardships.

3. **FBI Scams** – Perpetrators attempt to intimidate victims in emails by purporting to be high ranking government officials. Many scams exploit the FBI name or the names of FBI executives such as the current FBI Director, James Comey, and FBI former Director Robert Mueller, both of which had terms as the FBI's Director during 2013. There were 4,391 complaints reported to the IC3 in 2013 that referenced both FBI Directors. The FBI specific schemes typically remain the same as scammers just update their scam verbiage to reflect the current FBI Director's name. FBI impersonation schemes pose a viable threat to national security by undermining public trust that directly impacts law enforcement's ability to do its job. Government agencies do not send unsolicited e-mails of this nature.

While FBI, Department of Justice and other United States

government executives are briefed on numerous investigations, they do not personally contact consumers regarding such matters. United States government agencies use the legal process to contact individuals. These agencies do not send threatening letters or e-mails to consumers demanding payments for Internet crimes. The total FBI related scams reported to the IC3 during 2013 is represented in the chart below.

4. **Ransomware/Scareware Scams** – The IC3 has received multiple complaints surrounding ransomware /scareware schemes. These schemes are used to target and extort funds from victims by intimidating them. These scams began years ago with false claims in which the perpetrators pretended to be federal government officials who were watching or monitoring the victims' Internet usage. Schemes continue to change and some of the most reported schemes involve those discussed below.

Cryptolocker Ransomware – The IC3 became aware of the CryptoLocker scheme in October 2013. It spreads via e-mail and propagates rapidly. The virus encrypts various file types and then a pop-up window appears on victims' computer that states their data has been encrypted. The only way to get it back is to send a specified monetary payment to the perpetrator. This ransomware provides the victim with a timeline to pay via a displayed countdown clock. If victims do not pay on time, they lose the ability to pay and risk having their data permanently encrypted and rendered unusable. Perpetrators are demanding a $300 to $700 payment sent to the perpetrator using various methods.

Child Pornography Scareware – This scareware is transmitted when computer users visit an infected website. The victim's computer locks up and displays a warning that the user has violated U.S. federal law. Child pornography is either embedded in a banner image that appears on the victims' screen or revealed via an automatic browser redirecting them to a child pornography website. The scareware is used as an extortion technique by threatening prosecution for visiting or viewing these images. The victim is also informed that they have been recorded using audio, video and other devices. The only way to unlock the computer is to pay the fine, usually between $300 and $5,000.

Citadel Ransomware – The Citadel ransomware, named Reveton, displays a warning on the victims' computer purportedly from a law enforcement agency claiming that their computer had been used for illegal activities, such as downloading copyrighted software or child pornography. To increase the illusion they are being watched by law enforcement, the screen also displays the victim's IP address and some victims even report activity from their webcam. Victims are instructed to pay a fine to the U.S. Department of Justice to unlock their computer. Many were told to pay the fines via prepaid cash services such as Ucash or Paysafecard. In addition to installing the ransomware, the Citadel malware continues to operate on the compromised computer to collect sensitive data that could potentially be used to commit a variety of financial frauds.

In fact, the author himself was the victim of such an attack while working on this book. It occurred on a Sunday morning at about 07:00 when my computer suddenly went black and then a screen popped up, which included a photograph which had just been taken of me, sitting in bed!

It told me that I had committed one or other of several offences and mentioned breach of copyright downloading and visiting child pornography sites and that I was going to be prosecuted for a criminal offence. The site had logos of the Irish police force *An Garda Siochana*. It also told me that I could avoid criminal prosecution if I paid a fine and only then would by computer unfreeze. Having practiced law for twenty years I knew that neither the Irish Police Force or any other Police Force would seek to carry on in such a manner but what really threw me was the photograph that they had just taken of me, obviously through my webcam. In order to unfreeze my computer I had to borrow my daughter's laptop, google the scam and follow the instructions of someone else who had received the same scam. Thankfully his instructions worked.

Fake or Rogue Anti-Virus Software – In this scheme victims are scared into purchasing anti-virus software that would allegedly remove viruses from their computers. A pop-up box appears that informs users that their computers are full of viruses and need to be cleaned. The pop-up message has a button victims can click to purchase anti-virus software that supposedly can immediately get rid of these viruses. If the victims click the pop-up to purchase the anti-virus software, they are infected with malware. In some instances, victims have been infected regardless of clicking on the pop-up box.

5. **Hit Man Scam** – The IC3 continues to receive reports about a hit man/extortion e-mail scheme. The scheme has been around for several years but the content used in the e-mailed messages changes. The ultimate goal is for the perpetrators to defraud people through disturbing e-mails. The scam originated as a person sending an e-mail portraying himself as a hit man hired to kill the victim. The e-mail instructs the recipient to pay a fee to remain safe and avoid having the hit carried out. If you have been the victim of any of these scams you can make an on-line complaint to the FBI on their website www.ic3.gov. Just make sure it's not a counterfeit site!

15 DNA

While Francis Watson and James Crick of Cambridge University in England are credited with discovering DNA in April 1953 it was not until 1984 that Dr. Alec Jeffries of the Lister Institute of Leicester University developed the first DNA fingerprint. DNA was then successfully integrated into crime investigations by forensic serologists.

Serology refers to the study of serum, a clear yellow fluid found in separated whole blood and their work also extends to the analysis of semen, saliva, urine and other body fluids. There is no doubt that the discovery of DNA greatly increased the evidential value of their contribution to criminal investigations.

DNA is an incredibly complicated chemical made up of billions of parts called genes. Simply put, genes help to control different things in an individual's make-up like gender, height, hair, eye and skin color. We all inherit our DNA from our parents with exactly 50% derived from our mother and 50% derived from our father. Because there is such a vast number of possible ways that the genes in each half of the DNA can combine it is impossible for close relatives, even brothers and sisters to have exactly the same code. Only monozygous, that is, identical twins or clones share the same DNA.

SEROLOGY TESTS FOR BLOOD

Before a biological sample can be linked to a victim or a perpetrator the sample itself has to be identified. In many cases of traumatic death, blood will be one of the most important traces found at the scene and sent to the forensic laboratory for analysis. Various blood tests can greatly assist an investigation. One such test which is simple enough to be carried out at a basic lab or even at the crime scene is the Kastle-Meyer (KM) test. It is based on the fact that peroxidase enzymes in blood react with a chemical stain causing it to change color from clear to pink.

Another test which might be used is the precipitin test, sometimes called the Uhlenbuth test after the German scientist who developed it in 1901. This is an extremely sensitive test which only requires minute samples. Serum for the precipitin test is obtained from rabbits which have produced antibodies to destroy a small quantity of human blood injected into them.

A sample of the suspected human blood is placed on a gelatine coated slide next to a sample of the biological reagent (anti-serum). The serologist then passes an electric current through the glass by means of electrodes. This causes the protein molecules in the two samples to filter outwards through the gelatine towards each other. If a precipitin line forms, where the antigens and anti-bodies meet, the sample is human blood.

COLLECTING BLOOD

Blood that is in liquid pools is picked up on a gauze pad or other clean sterile cotton cloth. In cases where the stain is on some object or material the stained object should be delivered to the laboratory immediately or as soon as possible.

Here the stain should be allowed to air dry completely and then covered with a clean sheet of paper before packaging. Stained material should not be heated or placed in bright sunlight to dry. The clothing of the deceased should never folded across the stain, but should be folded so that the stain remains flat.

COLLECTING SEMEN

Semen stains are usually discovered on clothing, blankets, sheets, condoms, and couches. Semen stains discovered at the scene are allowed to air dry. Material is wrapped in clean paper, and packaged in paper bags, never plastic bags. A note should be made if the sample was wet when found. If there is sufficient quantity a liquid sample should also be taken before drying.

Again, clothing is never folded across the stain, but in such a way that the stain remains   flat. Semen stains on dark surfaces will be easily visible as a whitish stain. But if it has dried on a light colored surface it may be more difficult to detect so that examination using ultra violet light may be required. UV light will reveal the stain as a white or blue-white fluorescence.

The serologist will be aware that other substances such as urine produce a similar effect so the test may be invalid for articles of clothing such as undergarments. The identification of a sample as semen is usually carried out by way of a microscope which will display the spermacytes.

The Acid Phosphatase Color Test is used in the case of those suffering low or no sperm count or who have undergone a vasectomy. This test detects the presence of the acid phosphatase enzyme in semen, and although the enzyme is present in other body fluids, it is not present in such great concentration.

However, since this enzyme is present elsewhere in the body, the test cannot be regarded as absolute proof of the presence of semen on clothing or in material recovered in a case of suspected sexual assault. However detection of acid phosphatase amounts to powerful circumstantial evidence.

Not all bodily fluids will contain sufficient information to gain a DNA comparison as in the case of an individual who is a "non-secretor." Such a person will not have sufficient levels of protein in their bodily fluids to determine a match between blood and bodily fluids such as semen found at a crime scene. However, the percentage of non-secretors as opposed to secretors in the population is tiny. Semen is considered an excellent way to catch an offender and since 1984 many rapists have been convicted on the convincing evidence of their genetic fingerprint.

COLLECTING SALIVA

Saliva is a clear liquid, made and present in the mouth, which wets food making it easier to swallow. Additionally, specialized proteins that are present in saliva, such as salivary amylase, trigger chemical reactions that begin to break apart chemical bonds in the food. Saliva testing which is less obtrusive than obtaining blood or urine, is a good way of discovering drugs in the body.

It may also be present in sexual assault cases where biting or licking has occurred. The composition of the saliva accurately mirrors the proteins that are present in both the blood and the urine. While the current available methods for the screening of saliva in a forensic application are growing in number, they are not necessarily growing in popularity. The analyst is increasingly presented with the need to decide whether a pre-screening method would be worth the consumption of sample that could be applied for DNA analysis methods.

DNA TYPING

Typing is the detection of a person's genetic profile. Since 1985 forensic scientists have developed several different methods to process a DNA sample. All these methods require special equipment and chemicals, but the specific method used will depend on how large the sample is. The most common method used is the Short Tandem Repeat (STR) Analysis. Here, the serologist chemically highlights thirteen sections of human DNA which are then printed onto a sheet called a profile. Samples of DNA from several places can be printed onto the same profile to determine if they match.

DNA fingerprinting or DNA analysis includes any method used to analyze genes and DNA. This laboratory procedure is carried out in stages, the first of which is obviously the collection of specimens from the crime scene. The next stage is the extraction of the DNA from the nucleus of the cell. The cells could be from bodily fluids, blood, skin or hair.

Then the DNA needs to be isolated and cut so that it can be matched against other samples. Special enzymes recognize patterns in the DNA and cut the strand. Electrophoresis is the process used where the strands are placed on a gel where they are separated and an electric current passed through it. The results are compared against samples of all suspects and a match is determined.

Most countries now have a DNA database. In Britain DNA samples can be taken by the police from anyone arrested and detained in police custody in connection with a recordable offence. These include most offences other than traffic offences.

Two other types of samples retained are crime scene samples and volunteer samples (their consent is irrevocable). At present, samples and profiles may only be used for purposes related to preventing and detecting crime, investigating an offence, conducting a prosecution or identifying a deceased person or a body part.

THE PROBLEM WITH DNA

Contrary to what we see in programs like *CSI* it's not simply a question of a CS investigator using a swab an picking up a piece of DNA at a crime scene and matching it to the offender in twenty four hours. Where an offence is committed in a public place like a street or buildings vast amounts of DNA will be present in such areas because of the large numbers of people passing through every day.

Even in a confined area a large pool of blood could be contaminated with skin or hair that had fallen from someone who is not remotely connected with the crime. Another problem is that there will be increasing piles of evidence to be examined, much of it which may eventually turn out to have no bearing on the case under investigation.

Even where DNA is discovered it will take weeks to have it analyzed and even then the problem is finding a match. If the police do not already have the DNA of the offender in their database then they have no match.

So, contrary to popular belief and crime programs there is nothing magical about DNA. Certainly it is effective an many clod cases have been found because of DNA but it doesn't solve every crime. Many modern day serial killers like Dennis Rader have been convicted with the help of DNA.

16 COMMITTING THE PERFECT CRIME

"Our representation of the standard criminal might be based on the properties of those less intelligent ones who were caught."
— Nicholas Nassim Taleb, *The Black Swan*

How likely is a criminal to be caught? Well, it depends on the crime. According to the FBI 2010 figures the percentages are as follows:
Murder-Two out of three cases are solved.
Rape- Two out of five cases are solved.
Robbery- One out of five cases are solved.
Aggravated Assault- Fifty six per cent are caught.
Burglary- Only one in ten cases are solved.
Theft- One in five cases are solved.
Auto-Theft- One in ten cases are solved.

When you factor in the number of crimes that are not even reported then the clearance rate is much lower. For example, as many as fifty per cent of rape cases are not reported. This means the actual clearance rate is one in five.

One of the questions I am asked most is if it's possible to commit the perfect crime. When writing *Who's Who Serial Killers The Top 100* I was amazed by the sheer number of victims serial killers had murdered before they were ever caught. Dennis Rader stopped killing for years and would never have been caught had he not started writing to the media complaining about the lack of publicity they were giving him. If John Wayne Gacy had killed only 33 instead of 34 young men would he ever have been caught? The world's most famous serial killer, *Jack the Ripper*, was never caught. So, why is it that some people get caught and others get away with committing the perfect crime?

RELATIONSHIP

Let's take the crime of murder. It's so much easier to kill someone with whom you have no connection. You could go out tonight, drive into the city, shoot a homeless person sleeping on some deserted park bench and no one would ever know, or care. And the chances of you ever being caught are slim. Why? Two reasons: there is absolutely no connection between you and the homeless person and because, unfortunately, society doesn't really care about homeless people or even women who are obliged to resort to prostitution to feed their families.

And that is why most people get caught, connection. If you're planning on murdering your wife, don't. Why? Well, first of all it is morally and legally wrong, but also, you will be suspect *numero uno*. Remember the Locard Exchange Principle we talked about in Chapter 11? Every contact leaves a trace. The vast majority of murders are committed by those closest to the victim. The first person the police look at is the husband/wife/partner/associate/relative. Then they'll look at the motive. Were there financial difficulties in the relationship? Is their joint life cover? Is one of the parties having an affair? Did the couple argue? No matter how happy the relationship was there will always be someone close to the victim who will tell the police that things weren't always what they seemed. The majority of unsolved murder crimes are those committed by people who had no connection to the victim.

DNA

Offenders who break into someone's house and commit a crime are nearly always caught, because they leave behind fingerprints and some kind of DNA. Right? Wrong. Only one in ten get caught. Albert de Salvo aka *The Boston Strangler* committed hundreds of burglaries before he was caught. What about DNA? If you commit a crime in a place that is likely to have a lot of DNA from strangers like a shopping center, train station or park, finding your DNA will be like finding a needle in a haystack. Also, a really clever criminal might plant someone else's DNA at a crime site. If nothing else this will confuse the investigation. DNA is really only helpful to law enforcement agencies in murder and rape cases where the offender has left DNA on the victim and where the police already have his DNA on file.

Fingerprints are much more likely to connect an offender to a crime but most professional criminals wear thick gloves which leave no fingerprint trace. Where fingerprints have been left at a scene then a professional criminal will ensure to eradicate them properly. This will not mean a quick dust and wipe but using bleach and a heavy cloth.

COMPUTERS AND CELL PHONES

OK, so you're itching to commit a crime. Pick a crime, any crime, well, let's leave out anything that will involve computers. Why? Because in all crimes, particularly those involving computers there is always a trace. When you press "delete" on your computer, nothing is deleted. Ask Dr. Harold Shipman aka *Doctor Death*. Well, he committed suicide but had you asked him before he killed himself he would have said something like: "I don't understand how they know I changed the medical records of my victims. I pressed the delete button."

When you press "delete" it goes into your trash can. And when you open that and press "delete", nothing is deleted. It is just temporarily erased to give you space to overwrite it. But, it isn't gone. Trust me on this. If you really need to delete something on your computer then take it out to the back yard, buy a sledgehammer and smash it into little pieces. It still won't be deleted but at least it will be *Humpty Dumpty*, no one will be able to put the hard drive back together.

In fact, if you decide to commit a crime do not use your computer to help you. Why? Because even though you delete that internet browsing button every night, your history is still traceable, just like the messages on your cell phone. A professional criminal is unlikely to google stuff like "How to murder your wife" on their computer.

The same principle relates to cell phones. A professional is unlikely to use his cell phone if he is planning on committing a crime. His calls, messages and location can be traced. A clever criminal, like a drug dealer, will buy a pay-as-you-go-phone which is not registered to anyone and will change that phone and destroy the sim card every week.

WORKING WITH OTHERS

Don't. You want to rob a bank? Forget about it. Why? Because you can't do it on your own. You will need help. And that's the thing about crime. No matter how well you know your partner in crime the chances are they will rat you out in the end. So, the number one rule for seasoned criminals is, if you are going to commit a crime you do it on your own. The more people who know about the crime the greater the chance they will spill the beans. No one can be trusted forever. A person intent on committing a crime and determined not to get caught will choose one they can commit on their own.

PROXIMITY

The closer you live to the crime scene the greater your chance of getting caught. The ideal scenario for a professional is to travel to a different country, commit his crime, and return home. That way the local police will not have him in the frame. This is how most contract killings occur. The killer is in and out of the country usually before the crime is even discovered. If the crime is committed near to where he lives and if he is a suspect then the police will check his car and every vehicle to which he has access. They will check the mileage. They will examine CCTV of traffic monitors and all other CCTV coverage of the crime scene area. Many criminals, travelling locally, will opt to use public transport and travel in disguise.

TOOLS FOR THE CRIME

First of all, no professional will act like Dexter Morgan in *Dexter* who does the whole plastic-wrapped killer thing for every murder. Dexter probably doesn't know it but the manager from the store has already called the police like a million times already. "We have this guy who always buys yards of plastic and a shovel right before there's a major homicide in the city. I wonder if there's a connection?"

A clever criminal will buy whatever he needs to commit his crime at large department stores a long way from where he lives and only use cash. He will buy generic, very common brands and he will buy what he needs in different stores. He is unlikely to go into one store and buy a hunting knife, a balaclava and a shovel. He will shop in disguise in case he is picked up on CCTV store cameras and will immediately destroy any receipts, shopping bags or anything else that will connect him to those stores.

He will also destroy everything he had bought after the crime has been committed. Forensic pathologists are able to give exact dimensions of knives used in an attack from the victim's stab wounds. A case in point relates to the *BTK* killings. Police found a small knife in Dennis Rader's kitchen several years after he had used it in a murder. Finally, all these purchases will be made months in advance and not a few days before the crime.

EVIDENCE

Stupid criminals are caught because of the amount of evidence they leave behind. The golden rule is that if you have committed a crime don't try to hide the crime, hide your connection to the crime. What difference does it make if the police know the murder has been committed? If the crime involves a knife, a professional will drop it at the scene. If it involves a gun, some will leave it at the scene but others will drop it in a lake. Both scenarios have risks. Ballistic experts can nearly always trace the origin of a gun and connect it to other crimes in which it has been used. A gun which has been dropped in a lake or the sea is unlikely ever to be found but the risk is in being caught with the gun on your person before you dispose of it.

Most criminals are caught not because they committed the crime but because they try to cover it up. If they have murdered someone there is no point in moving the body or chopping off the head and burying it somewhere. The resulting torso may make it difficult to identify but the probability of trace evidence existing when the head, hands or other body parts are transported to another location will be high. Similarly, if they have stolen something a seasoned thief will dispose of it immediately. If they have stolen a large amount of cash they are not going to go out and buy a new Porsche, nor deposit it in their local bank.

THE GETAWAY

A criminal leaving the scene of a crime will be conscious of the omnipresent use of CCTV cameras. They are everywhere, in and outside stores and on traffic pylons.

Once you hit the main road the chances are that you will be on camera for your entire journey. Many criminals will avoid main roads and travel by motorcycle or bicycle. They might travel very late at night or early in the morning and always have an excuse if they are stopped. They will always destroy all the clothes they were wearing during the commission of a crime often by burning them and thoroughly shower immediately afterwards.

THE ALIBI

A good alibi is essential. A lot of ex-cons try to have someone else given them an alibi. This is not a good idea. Firstly, it involves someone else, usually a completely innocent third party, in the crime. Secondly, when it comes to the crunch and they realize that they could be charged in relation to a crime they didn't even know about they will often capitulate and testify against the offender. A professional criminal will create his own alibi.

A professional hitman is likely to plan a trip out of town at the time of the crime. He will book a rental car and a hotel with his credit card. He might even sign up for a convention, film or music festival which he will attend momentarily and blend in. It's possible he might even take a few selfies to prove he was there. But he will use a hotel with no cameras and little security. He will use his mobile phone to make calls from that location, leave to commit the crime and return as soon as possible. He will probably have rented a movie in the hotel which will be running at the time of the crime.

CRIME AFTERMATH

Professional criminals will avoid all television and media exposure to their crime. They will not advertise the spoils of their crime, nor will they talk about the crime to anyone.

If they are brought in for questioning they will remain silent. They know that the police require evidence, even if they confess. The chances are that the police haven't got it. They certainly haven't got the evidence if they haven't charged anyone. They may and probably will suspect and try to get the offender to confess.

They will tell them that they have the evidence; that they can connect them to the crime; that's it's only a matter of time before they have enough to charge them; that it will be better for them to confess now and save themselves a long stretch in prison; and, that their partner/lover/husband/wife has already indicated their guilt. They will even adopt the good cop-bad cop routine but if the suspect doesn't confess then they won't be charged unless they have made some bad errors of judgment or not read this book properly.

Even if the police have evidence it may not be enough to secure a conviction. The prosecution must prove the case "beyond a reasonable doubt." This is a particularly high standard and the prosecution know that anything can go wrong for them during the trial. This is the reason why they are usually willing to plea bargain, like for example, accepting a plea to manslaughter instead of the more serious crime of murder.

Is there ever any communication in chambers between the prosecution and a sitting judge during a trial? This type of practice would be totally inappropriate. But to answer your question: you might say so but I couldn't possibly comment.

17 GLOSSARY OF TERMS

Acarology: The study of mites and ticks.

Accelerants: Any chemical that can start fires and explosions quickly.

Acetysalics: Aspirin based drugs.

Algenate: A plaster like compound.

Amino acids: Amino acids play central roles both as building blocks of proteins and as intermediates in metabolism.

Analyte: The substance in an analysis that is being identified or determined.

Anatomy: The science that studies the structure of the body.

Aneurysm: A localized widening (dilatation) of an artery, vein, or the heart. At the area of an aneurysm there is typically a bulge and the wall is weakened and may rupture.

Aniline dyes: Any of a large number of synthetic dyes derived from aniline, usually obtained from coal tar.

Anthropology: The scientific study of the origin, the behavior, and the physical, social, and cultural development of humans.

Anthropometry: The measurement of the size and proportions of the human body.

Antibodies: Vital elements in the body's immune system and are secreted by the white-blood cells.

Archaeology: The systematic study of past human life and culture by the recovery and examination of remaining material evidence.

Asphyxia: Insufficient oxygen in the blood.

Asymmetry: The condition of an animal body in which there is no plane which would divide the body into two similar halves.

Auditory meatus: The ear canal that runs from the outer ear to the middle ear.

Autopsy: A special surgical operation, performed by specially-trained physicians, on a dead body. Its purpose is to learn the truth about the person's health during life, and how the person really died.

Ballistics: The study of the functioning of firearms, the flight of the bullet, and the effects of different types of ammunition.

Barbiturates: Synthetic sedatives.

Bore: The hole through the middle of the gun barrel.

Breech: The part of the barrel at the back of the gun into which the bullets are loaded.

Calibre: The diameter of the bore of a gun taken as a unit of measurement.

Carbon monoxide: An odorless, colorless, non-irritant gas formed when carbon is oxidized in a limited supply of air.

Cauterisation: The application of heat, mechanically or

chemically, to prevent or stop bleeding.

Chromotography: A method of separating and identifying the components of a complex mixture by differential movement through a two-phase system, in which the movement is effected by a flow of a liquid or a gas (mobile phase) which percolates through an adsorbent (stationary phase) or a second liquid phase.

Clones: A cell, group of cells, or organism that is descended from and genetically identical to a single common ancestor.

Computer tomography: Computer analysis of a series of cross-sectional scans made along a single axis.

Conjunctivae: The membranes connecting the inner eye lids to the eyeballs.

Coroner: A government official appointed to investigate (conduct an inquest into) the causes and circumstances of sudden, suspicious, or violent deaths. A coroner's court is a fact finding and not a prosecuting body.

Cyanoacrylate: Superglue.

De-calcification: To remove calcium or calcium compounds from bones or teeth.

Dentition: The type, number, and arrangement of a set of teeth.

Dimorphism: Two distinct forms within a single species, e.g. visual differences between genders.

Dioxyribonucleic acid (DNA): One of two types of molecules that encode genetic information. The other is

RNA. In humans DNA is the genetic material; RNA is transcribed from it. In some other organisms, RNA is the genetic material, and in reverse fashion, the DNA is transcribed from it.

Double helix: The structure of DNA with the two strands of DNA spiraling about one other.

Eccrine glands: Sweat glands, responsible for most of the body's temperature control.

Ejector: The mechanism in a firearm that ejects the empty cartridge or shell after firing.

Entomology: The study of insects and related arthropods.

Ethanol: Ethyl alcohol.

Extractor: A fitting in many firearms for removing spent cartridges from the chamber.

Firing pin: That part in the bolt or breech of a firearm which strikes the primer and explodes the charge.

Fluor: A flowing; so called from its use as a flux.

Fluorescence: The emission of electromagnetic radiation, especially of visible light.

Forensic anthropology: The application of the science of physical anthropology to the legal process. Forensic anthropology includes the identification of skeletal, decomposed, or unidentified human remains.

Forensic botany: The application of plant science to the resolution of legal questions.

Forensic entomology: The use of the insects and their arthropod relatives that inhabit decomposing remains to aid legal investigations.

Forensic science: The scientific analysis and documentation of evidence suitable for legal proceedings.

Formaldehyde (HCHO): A colorless gas, soluble in water, used as an antiseptic, in embalming and the manufacture of synthetic resins.

Gas chromatography: A chromatographic technique that can be used to separate organic compounds that are volatile.

Genes: The basic physical unit of heredity.

Grooves and lands: A barrel for rifles and pistols is equipped with lands and grooves, wherein the greatest measure of the groove caliber of the barrel corresponds with the minimum measure of the diameter of the projectile, and the land caliber amounts to about 96 percent of the groove caliber. The grooves are the spaces that are cut out, and the resulting ridges are called lands. It is the lands that cut into the bullet and impart spin.

Gum Arabic: A water-soluble, gummy exudate obtained from the acacia tree, especially Acacia senegal, used as an emulsifier, an adhesive, in inks, and in pharmaceuticals

Hemorrhage: Bleeding.

Instar: A period of growth of insect larvae, ending with a moult.

Lands: The raised areas between grooves in gun barrels.

Larvae: An immature form or stage of an animal following the egg – in insects it is a wormlike or grublike stage of the complete metamorphosis.

Larynx: The organ of the voice located between the trachea and the base of the tongue.

Latent fingerprints: A fingerprint that is not apparent to the eye but can be made sufficiently visible, as by dusting or fuming, for use in identification.

Ligature: A cord, wire, or bandage used for tying or binding.

Liver mortis: Also known as lividity or hypostasis. It is a term used to describe the draining of the blood to lower portions of the body due to the influence of gravity. The body develops a patchy discoloration within 1-2 hours of death and the process is complete within 6-12 hours.

Luminescence: The emission of light not caused by incandescence and occurring at a temperature below that of incandescent bodies.

Lycopodium powder: A fine powder or dust composed of the spores of Lycopodium, and other plants of the order Lycopodiaceæ. It is highly inflammable, and is sometimes used in the manufacture of fireworks, and the artificial representation of lightning.

Mandible: The lower jaw of a vertebrate animal.

Mass spectroscopy: The use of spectroscopy to determine the masses of small electrically charged particles.

Mastoid: A large, bony prominence on the base of the skull behind the ear, containing air spaces that connect with the middle ear cavity.

Maxillary bones: Either of a pair of irregularly shaped bones of the skull, fusing in the midline, supporting the upper teeth, and forming part of the eye sockets, hard palate, and nasal cavity; upper jaw.

Meiotic: The process of cell division in sexually reproducing organisms that reduces the number of chromosomes in reproductive cells from diploid to haploid, leading to the production of gametes in animals and spores in plants.

Metabolite: A chemical substance in the body that is the product of change or breakdown of another substance by the body's chemical "machinery."

Metamorphosis: Transformation; Change of shape.

Monozygous (identical) twins: Twins that originate from a single fertilised egg (a zygote).

Morphology: The branch of biology that deals with the form and structure of organisms without consideration of function.

Musculature: The system or arrangement of muscles in a body or a body part.

Ninhydrin: A chemical reagent used for the detection and analysis of primary amines, especially amino acids, with which it forms a derivative with an intense purple color.

Occiput: The back of the head or skull of vertebrates.

Olein oil: A liquid glyceride, $(CHCO)CH$, present in olive oil and certain other oils and fats

Organic solvents: Are a chemical class of compounds that are used routinely in commercial industries. They share a common structure (at least 1 carbon atom and 1 hydrogen atom), low molecular weight, lipophilicity, and volatility, and they exist in liquid form at room temperature.

Ossification: The natural process of bone formation. The hardening or calcification of soft tissue into a bone-like material.

Osteology: The branch of anatomy that deals with the structure and function of bones.

Oxidising agents: A substance that oxidizes another substance, being itself reduced in the process. Common oxidizing agents are oxygen, hydrogen peroxide, and ferric salts.

Palaeontology: The study of the forms of life existing in prehistoric or geologic times, as represented by the fossils of plants, animals, and other organisms.

Palynology: The scientific study of spores, pollen and certain algae.

Patent fingerprints: Fingerprints that are immediately visible to the naked eye.

Pathology: The scientific study of the nature of disease and its causes, processes, development, and consequences.

Peroxidase enzymes: An enzyme occurring especially in plants, milk, and white blood cells and consisting of a protein complex with hematin groups that catalyzes the oxidation of various substances by peroxides.

pH: A measure of the acidity or alkalinity of a solution, numerically equal to 7 for neutral solutions, increasing with increasing alkalinity.

Phoresy: A relationship between two different species of organisms in which the larger, or host, organism transports a smaller organism, the guest.

Piezo electricity: The generation of electricity or of electric polarity in dielectric crystals subjected to mechanical stress, or the generation of stress in such crystals subjected to an applied voltage.

Poison: Any substance which when introduced into the body causes death.

Polyethylene glycol: Any of a family of colorless liquids with high molecular weight that are soluble in water and in many organic solvents and are used in detergents and as emulsifiers and plasticizers.

Polygraph: A machine that measures a person's reactions, sometimes known as a lie detector.

Post mortem: An examination of a corpse in order to determine cause of death.

Precipitates: Solids formed in a solution or inside another solid during a chemical reaction.

Precipitin: An antibody that reacts with a specific soluble antigen to produce a precipitate.

Presumptive tests: A simple test for a given substance using a reagent that changes color when mixed with the substance under investigation.

Puparium: The hard pupal case of the insect pupa.

Pupate: To go through a pupal stage.

Putrefaction: The decomposition of animal or vegetable matter in the absence of oxygen by microbes.

Ramus of the mandible: One of the two prominent, projecting back parts of the horseshoe-shaped lower jaw bone.

Reamed: A finished hole that had already been roughly drilled. The end product of an operation from which is expected a certain level of dimensional and geometric quality, as well as a smooth surface condition.

Riboflavin: Riboflavin, or vitamin B2, is a member of the water-soluble family of B-complex vitamins. It is required for glucose metabolism so that the body can produce energy from carbohydrates, normal red blood cell production and general body growth.

Rifled: The inside of a gun barrel which is grooved with spiral channels to give the bullet a rotary motion, thus ensuring greater accuracy of fire.

Rigor mortis: Stiffening of the body muscles after death.

Serology: The study and examination of bodily fluids that is used in forensic science as a means of segregating fluids excreted by assailants or attackers in varying criminal acts. These acts can range from physical assault to sexual assault, right through to the act of murder and all of them will have an element of fluid secretion attached to them.

Solvents: A substance, usually a liquid, capable of dissolving another substance

Spectroscopy: The measurement of the absorption, scattering, or emission of electromagnetic radiation by atoms or molecules.

Spermatocyte: A cell that undergoes the first meiotic division in male.

Striation marks: Lines or grooves left on a bullet as a result of its passage through the barrel of the weapon which fired it.

Taxonomy: The science of classifying and naming living organisms.

Toxicology: The science dealing with poisons and their effects and with antidotes for poisons.

Toxin: A poison that is produced by bacterial pathogens and that damage cells

Tranquiliser: A drug that acts on the central nervous system and is used to calm, decrease anxiety, or help a person to sleep.

Thin layer chromatography: Type of chromatography using as the stationary phase a thin layer (0.01 inch [0.25 mm]) of a special finely ground matrix (silica gel, alumina, or similar material) coated on a glass plate or incorporated in a plastic film.

18 BIBLIOGRAPHY

Beavan C. (2003) Fingerprints London: Fourth Estate

Beres, D.B. Prokos. A (2008) Crime Scene: Profilers and Poison New York:Scholastic

Byrd, J.; Castner. J.L. (2009) Forensic Entomology: Utility of Arthropods in Legal Investigations London:Taylor & Francis

Cowling, P. (2008) Guidelines for Handling Medicolegal Specimens and Preserving the Chain of Evidence London: Royal College of Pathologists – Institute of Biomedical Science.

Dale, W. M. Becker, W. S.(2007) The Crime Scene:How Forensic Science Works New York:Kaplan Publishing

Erer S. Duzbakar O. Demirhan & Erdemir A. (2006) 'A Forensic Autopsy Case Belonging to the 19th Century in Turkey' Bursa (Turkey): Uludag University

Erzinclioglu, Z. (2004) Forensics True Crime Scene Investigations London:Carlton

Erzinclioglu, Z. (2006) Forensics London: Carlton

Evans. C, (1996) The Casebook of Forensic Detection Chichester:John Wiley & Sons

Ferllini, R. (2002) Raising the Dead London: John Blake Publishing Ltd.

Fisher B.A.J. Fisher D.R. & Kolowski J. (2007) Forensics DeMystified New York : McGraw-Hill

Frith A. (2007) Forensic Science London : Usborne Publishing Ltd.

Garrett, G. Nott, A. (2001) Cause of Death London: Robinson

Goff, M.L. (1996) A Fly for the Prosecution:How Insects Help Solve Crimes Cambs (Mass.) :Havard University Press.

Hechtlinger, A. (1961) Modern Science Dictionary (ed) W Abbot London: Chatto & Windus

Horn, S. (2005) The Restless Sleep London:Bantam Books

Lane, B. (1992) The Encyclopedia of Forensic Science London: Headline Publishing

McBrewster J (2009) Forensic Entomology: Arthropod, Insect, Home stored product entomology, Francesco Redi, Jean Pierre Mégnin, Decomposition, Forensic entomological decomposition, Insect development during storage. eds. F.P. Miller, A.F. Vandome and J. McBrewster Alphascript Publishing

Menzell, E.R. Duff, J.M. (1979) "Laser Detection of Latent Fingerprints—Treatment with Fluorescers" in Journal of Forensic Sciences Vol.24(1) January 1979

Miller, H. (1998) Forensic Fingerprints London:Headline Books

Miller Coyle, H. Lung Lee,C Yu Lin, W Lee1,H.C. & Palmbac, T.M. (2005) "Forensic Botany: Using Plant Evidence to Aid in Forensic Death Investigation" in Croat Medical Journal46(4) pp606 -612.

NPIA (2010) National Fingerprint Database available online at www.npia.police.uk/en/10504.htm

Prag, J, Neave, R. (1997) Making faces using forensic and archaeological evidence. London:British Museum Press,

Ricciuti E. (2007) Science 101:Forensics New York : Harper Collins

Roland, P. (2007) Crime Scenes London:Arcturus
Siegel J. (2009) Forensic Science Oxford : One World Publications

Segal, J. (2009) Forensic Science Oxford:One World Publications

Selfox P (2009) Criminal Investigation Cullompton: Willan Publishing

Stewart, C. P., and A. Stolman (eds.). Toxicology, Mechanisms and Analytical Methods. Vol. 1. Academic Press, New York, 1961, pp. 1-18.

Vanezis, M., and P. Vanezis. "Cranio-Facial Reconstruction in Forensic Identification—Historical Development and a Review of Current Practice." Medicine, Science, and the Law, 40 (July 2000): 197–205.

Ward. J, (1998) Crime Busting London:Blandford

Wilkinson, C. (2004) Forensic facial reconstruction. Cambridge: University Press,

Wilson, C. Wilson, D. (2003) Written in Blood London: Constable & Robinson Ltd

ABOUT THE AUTHOR

David Elio Malocco was born in Dundalk, County Louth, Ireland. His father was born in Casalattico in Frosinone in Italy and his mother was born in Monaghan in Ireland. He was educated at the Christian Brothers School in Dundalk and his parents later sent him to St. Patricks College in Cavan where they hoped he would be ordained as a Catholic priest. But he chose law and business instead.

He received his Bachelor of Civil Law degree from University College Dublin and spent fifteen years as a criminal lawyer before taking a second degree at the Open University, Milton Keynes in England where he obtained a first class honors degree in Psychology majoring in Cognitive Development.

In 1991 he realized a personal ambition and moved to New York where he studied film direction, production and writing for film at New York University. Since then he has written numerous screenplays in several genre and has written, produced and directed many shorts and three feature films, *Virgin Cowboys*, *Magdalen* and *Jack Gambel: The Enigma*.

He later studied creative writing at Oxford University and is presently completing a doctorate of divinity in Metaphysical Science. He is a member of the American Society of Criminology. He has written four books on serial killers: *Serial Sex Killers, Real American Psychos; Sexual Psychopaths, British Serial Killers; Murder for Profit, and Who's Who Serial Killers the Top 100*. The books were motivated by dual diplomas he had taken in the Psychology of Criminal Profiling and the second in Forensic Science specializing in Crime Scene Analysis.

He lives with his family in London, England.

Made in the USA
Lexington, KY
13 September 2015